Designing Creative Materials For Young Children

JUDY HERR
YVONNE LIBBY
University of Wisconsin—Stout

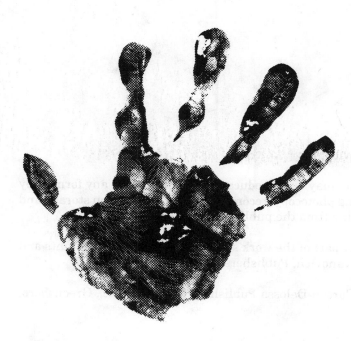

Harcourt Brace Jovanovich, Publishers
San Diego   New York   Chicago   Austin   Washington, D.C.
London   Sydney   Tokyo   Toronto

Pages 58, 106, 134, 270, 274 are courtesy of Carson-Delossa Publishing Company, Inc., Greensboro, North Carolina.

ISBN: 0-15-517361-8

Library of Congress Catalog Card Number: 89-84253

Printed in the United States of America

All photographs by Martin Springer.

Preface

Designing Creative Materials for Young Children contains ideas, instructions, and photographs of materials made by teachers to promote the emotional, social, physical, and cognitive development of young children. These educational materials have been designed to encourage initiative and curiosity through active exploration and interaction with other children and/or adults. Such interaction should produce meaningful learning experiences for young children.

All of the creative, teacher-made materials in the book have been used successfully in children's programs in the Child and Family Study Center at the University of Wisconsin-Stout. The majority of the materials were placed in learning centers and made available as choices for the children to explore and manipulate during large blocks of time referred to as self-selected play periods. Many of the materials offer the child a choice of solitary activity or of participating in a small group.

Ideas are included for art, dramatic play, language arts, large motor, math, music, room environment, science, sensory, small motor, social studies, and the writing center. The instructions for each teaching aid contain:

- classroom interest areas where the material(s) can be used.

- themes that the material complements

- goals for the teacher indicating the developmental value for children

- materials and tools needed for constructing the teacher aid(s)

- a step-by-step explanation of how to construct each aid

- teaching/learning strategies for introducing and/or effectively using materials with a group of young children.

This book represents ideas that have been gleaned from our experiences in teaching young children and in educating teachers of young children in a university setting. While it is impossible to recognize all of the individuals who encouraged us to share our ideas, we would be remiss in not acknowledging the following individuals: Carla Ahmann, Mary Babula, Terry Bloomberg, Margaret Brunn, Diane Carriveau, Carol Davenport, Jill Davis, Linda DeMoe, Rita Pittman Devery, Donna Dixon, Harriet Egertson, Judy Gifford, Nancy Gowan, Nancy Graese, Bessie Gray, Sue Herbach, Patti Herman, Joan Herwig, Paula Iverson, Judy Jax, Angela LaBonne Kaiser, Beth Libby, Janet Maffet, Janet Massea, Ginny McCaig, Katie McCarthy, Nancy McCarthy, Cindy Merde, Julie Meyers, Teresa Mitchell, Robin Muza, Kelli Railton, Lori Singerhouse Register, Peg Saienga, Kathy Rucker Schaeffer, Cheryl Smith, Karen Stepens, and Mary Eileen Zenk.

INTRODUCTION

This introduction will provide an explanation for each of the sections in the book. It also includes theme suggestions and a list of common materials that can be saved and used for making classroom materials.

SECTION ORGANIZATION

Designing Creative Materials for Young Children is divided into 12 curriculum areas commonly found in early childhood programs: art, dramatic play, language arts, large motor, math, music, room environment, science, sensory, small motor, social studies, and writing centers. Many of the materials in the section on room environment are decorative, as well as educational.

Art

Art provides children with an opportunity to do original planning and thinking. The process of dealing with art involves the senses and imagination. The creative, teacher-made materials in this book are designed to encourage creative expression and foster experimentation with art media. Children take pleasure and learn while manipulating and changing materials. Through the construction and use of the Crayon/Marker "Bundles," children can, for example, experiment with cause-and-effect relationships. The materials in this section, like all of the others, are designed to promote growth and development. Most of the art activities promote eye–hand coordination skills, provide for self-expression, and develop small muscle skills. And some of the materials—Chunk Crayons, the Colored-Sand Chart, and Paint Pallets—reinforce color recognition and appreciation skills. Additionally, the Squeeze-Bottle Art Chart creates an awareness of changes in substances.

Dramatic Play

Dramatic play provides children with an opportunity to try out new roles and to make decisions. While imitating others, children learn to understand fears and fantasies by expressing them. Furthermore, through this process, they are able to clarify concepts. To promote role-playing, this section offers Dance Tutus, Yarn Wigs, Paper Bag Costumes, Insect Costumes, Bird Masks, and Bunny Ears. Additionally, the Clown Makeup Chart allows children to experiment with cause-and-effect relationships. The Restaurant Menus, Washing Machine and Dryer, Gas Pump, Dramatic-Play Signs, Car Wash, and Ice-Cream Parlor Props are all materials designed to provide opportunities for role-playing. As the children learn to cooperate and share these materials, social and language skills may also be developed.

Language Arts

Carefully selected language arts materials promote development in listening, speaking, and writing. The Alphabet Book is designed to promote the identification of letters. Letters make words, and words are the focus of The Rhyming Word Train materials which promote the development of auditory association skills and the learning of new words. Through words children learn to describe their experiences and feelings and to develop a relationship between the printed word and the spoken word. Puppets are a powerful medium for encouraging children to dramatize their thoughts and feelings. While using a puppet, children lose themselves by becoming the character(s). Pot-holder Puppets, Pop-Up Puppets, Nylon Masks, Mouse Finger Puppets, Hamburger-Box Puppet, Glove Puppets, and an Elephant are all included in this section to encourage dramatization skills. A Magnetic Puppet Stage and Story "TV" Box are included to encourage the use of puppets. (Although a stage is desirable, it is not always necessary.)

Large Motor

The large motor materials included in this book are designed for use indoors or outdoors. The six teacher-made materials in this section promote the development of coordination skills. These materials also promote other skills: Balloon Bat, Dowel Horse, and Hopscotch Mat foster cooperation; Movement Wands encourages creative movement and self-expression; Footprints promote color identification and individual choices; and Creative Elastics introduces problem-solving.

Math

The focus of math materials for young children should be exploration, discovery, and understanding. The concepts of color, classification, measurement, position, volume, and number recognition all need to be included in a well-structured environment. Because color is considered a mathematical activity, the teacher-made materials focusing on color help young children to discriminate among objects. Our Favorite-Colors Chart and Ice-Cream Cone Match have been designed to promote color awareness. The Floor Shape Puzzle has been designed to promote problem-solving and color-identification skills. And the Favorite-Vegetable Chart provides an opportunity for children to engage in classification—sorting or grouping objects into categories or classes by some distinguishing characteristic.

Counting is another basic math skill that needs to be included in the curriculum. It is an important problem-solving tool, and several materials have been included to encourage counting and to promote numeral recognition skills. Examples include the Apple-and-Worm Match, Apple-Trees Flannel Board Match, Baseball Glove Match, Dog-and-Folder Game, Fishing Fun, Football-and-Clothespin Match, Halloween Ghosts Folder Game, Snowpeople-and-Hats Match, Valentine Folder Game, Watermelon-and-Plate Matching, Plastic-Eggs-and-Pom-Pom Match.

Music

Laughter, creativity, enjoyment, freedom, and movement are all encouraged by music. It is a universal language expressed through voice and body. Music can teach listening skills, differences in sounds, and language patterns. Children can also develop an appreciation of their cultural heritage through music. In addition to musical skills, three of the teacher-made materials in this section—Little Red Wagon, Color Paddles, and Five Green-Speckled Frogs—also promote color recognition. The Color-Coded Song Charts are designed to encourage children to play the keys on a musical instrument such as a piano, an organ, or tune bells. The colored circles on these charts should match those pasted onto the keys of a musical instrument. A teaching aid is also included for introducing the song "Old MacDonald." To promote rhythm skills, Wrist Bells, Rhythm Sticks, and Rhythm Cards for "1, 2 Buckle My Shoe" are included. A teaching aid has also been developed to teach a favorite song of young children, "The Wheels On the Bus."

Room Environment

The teacher-made materials in the classroom environment section communicate to children, parents, and other teachers what is expected of them and what is happening in the classroom. A well-planned environment is inviting, interesting, and conveys a message. To assist the teacher in decorating the room, four materials related to birthdays are included: Birthday Balloons, Birthday Cakes, Birthday Packages, and Birthday Train. Clock Decorations have been included for each month of the year, and a Daily Schedule Chart has been designed to encourage an awareness of the daily classroom routine. Car Pool Signs have been included to communicate to both staff and parents the names of children in each car pool. The Number of Children Per Area has been included to promote the development of self-control by setting clear limits. A Book-Return Box has been included in the book to help children learn how to care for books and to encourage cooperative behavior. The Labels for Classroom Areas or Centers offer the message that writing and reading are meaningful. The Number-Line Calendar promotes an awareness of time. And to coordinate home and school practices, a Parent

Space has been designed for the classroom. Finally, responsibility for belongings is encourage through a Lost-And-Found Box.

Science

Children must actively explore and question to understand their world, and science helps them learn to do that. As children observe, wonder, and ask questions, they learn science and develop general knowledge and language skills. Materials in this section are designed to encourage the development of imagination and curiosity. A Felt Weather Recorder is included in this section to foster an understanding of the effects of different weather conditions. To encourage children to develop prediction skills, a chart entitled Things That Move When Blown With A Straw is included. Hand Rests have been designed to encourage safety awareness during cooking activities. To track the passage of time, Hatching-Eggs Countdown is included. A Height-and-Weight Chart is included to promote the concepts of height and weight. Paintbrush-and-Bucket Color Match, Pail-and-Shovel Color Match, and Colored Glasses are all materials developed to introduce and/or review color identification skills. To develop an appreciation for living things, a Leaf Book and Terrarium are included. To introduce the relationship of temperature to weather this section contains a Temperature Graph. The Thermometer also reinforces weather concepts and introduces the new vocabulary words *fahrenheit* and *centigrade*. Instruction for making a Wave Jar are included. Other creative teacher-made materials in this section include a Worm-Farm Chart, Sink-or-Float Chart, Marble Track Game, Absorption Chart, Orange-Shake Recipe Chart, Insect Net, Carrot-Cake Recipe Chart, Circle-Glider Chart, Frog Life Cycle, Reflection Cards, and Magic Mirror Pictures.

Sensory

Through the exploration of materials, children learn many concepts—color, shape, and size, for example. Through "hands on" experimentation, sensitivity to tactile and visual experiences are improved. This section includes two bubble charts—Bubble Recipe Chart and Bubble-Prints Chart. The teacher-made materials for the Individual Feely Box, Scoops, Sifters, and Goop Chart have been designed to promote tactile awareness. Fingerpainting In A Bag encourages self-expression.

Small Motor

A variety of teacher-made materials have been included to foster small motor skills. The Wrapping-Paper Lotto Game makes an excellent addition to the game center. It can be played individually, with another child or the teacher, or in small groups. The Lacing Cards, Egg-Shaped Wallpaper Puzzles, and Valentine Puzzle are excellent activities for self-directed or self-initiated play. And The Rainbow-Chain Chart is an excellent small motor activity which also fosters color-recognition and sequencing skills. The Leaf Concentration Game, Snowflake Chart and Sticker Dominoes are also designed to practice following directions.

Social Studies

Young children need to build socialization skills by experiencing the people around them. And to become effective citizens it is necessary to understand the social symbols of our society. The teacher-made materials in this section are designed to introduce social study concepts. The Traffic Light is designed to associate color with action. The purpose of the Road Map For Small Cars and Trucks and Helper Chart is to promote helping and cooperation. Traditional Halloween symbols can be introduced through "The Goblin In the Dark" Game Pieces. Birthday Crowns, Community-Helpers Body Puppets, Farm Lotto Game, and "The Farmer In The Dell" Game Pieces all promote social skills.

Writing Center

The writing center is an important classroom area. It promotes letter-recognition skills, encourages fine motor coordination skills, fosters hand–eye coordination skills, and promotes an interest in the written word. "The Apple Tree Chart" and "A Chubby Little Snowman Chart" can be hung in this area to add aesthetic appeal to the room and promote exposure to the printed word. Alphabet Cards for Playdough can be constructed to promote letter recognition skills. And Wipe-Off Postcards and Wipe-Off Cards can provide opportunities for concrete learning experiences. Water color markers, grease pencils, or crayons may be used to write or draw on these cards. Letter-recognition skills can also be stimulated through such materials as Object-and-Word Cards, Tactile Letters, and Dried-Glue-Rubbings.

MATERIAL ORGANIZATION

Each material has the same consistent format: Interest Areas, Themes, Teacher's Goals, Preparation, Teaching/Learning Strategies, and Resources.

Interest Areas

Interest areas, which may be referred to as centers or activity areas in some programs, are defined as space for play. This book contains teacher-made materials for the art, dramatic play, language arts, large motor, math, music, science, sensory, small motor, social studies, and writing areas. In addition, materials have been designed to make the classroom environment more responsive and attractive.

Themes

The materials all have themes, sometimes referred to as units, concepts, or general ideas. For example, a theme on colors could be developed using the following teacher-made curriculum materials described in the book:

Chunk Crayons	Yarn Wigs
Colored-Sand Chart	Surprise Bags
Crayon/Marker "Bundles" Chart	Football Clothespin Match
Deodorant Bottle Painting	Floor Shape Puzzle
Paint Pallets	Our Favorite Color Chart
Squeeze Bottle Art Chart	Footprints To Follow
	Color-Coded Song Charts

Hopscotch Mat
Little Red Wagon
Color Paddles
Colored Glasses
Pail-and-Shovel   Color
    Match
Paintbrush-and-Bucket
    Color Match

Fingerpainting In A Bag
Goop Chart
Bubble Print Chart
Birthday Balloons
Color Crayons
Lacing Cards
Traffic Light

A variety of themes can be taught with a single teacher-made material. Paper Bag Costumes, for example, relate to the following themes: Actors/actresses, occupations, Halloween, farm animals, fairy tales, and communication. A total of 120 themes are listed in the text. Included are:

Acting
Air
Animals
Apples
Art
Auto Mechanic
Ballet
Balls
Bells
Birds
Birthdays
Bones
Books
Boxes
Brushes
Bubbles
Cars and Trucks
Celebrations
Chickens
Christmas
Circus
Clothes or Clothing
Colors
Communication
Community Helpers
Cooking
Costumes
Counting
Containers
Creativity
Dance
Designs
Easter
Exercise
Fairy Tales
Fall
Fasteners
Farm Animals
Feelings

Food(s)
Friends
Frogs
Fruits
Games
Gardens
Gloves
Hair Stylist
Halloween
Health
Hobbies
Holidays
Horses
Hot/Cold
Insects
Insects and Spiders
Instruments
Laundromat
Leaves
Letters
Library
Light
Masks
My Body
My Center
Music
Measurement
Me, I'm Special
Movement
Numbers
Nursery Rhymes
Nutrition
Occupations
Ocean
Our Senses
Paper
Painting
Pets
Pictures

Plants	Signs
Poetry	Sports
Puppets	Stores
Puzzles	Stories
Rabbits	Storytelling
Rhymes	Summer
Restaurant	Symbols
Recipes	Tools
Safety	Touch
Sand and Soil	Transportation
Science	Trees
Scissors	Valentine's Day
Seasons	Water
Seeds	Weather
Senses	Winter
Self-Concept	Wild Animals
Shapes	Wheels
Shovels and Scoops	Words
Sight	Writing
Sink/Float	Writing Tools
Sounds	Zoo

Teacher's Goals

The teacher goals in this book include the "why" or value, of the materials. For example, by introducing the Washer and Dryer material the teacher will:

- provide opportunities for role playing.

- promote the social skill of cooperation.

- develop an awareness of household tasks.

Preparation

This section lists all of the resources you will need to make each material. To save time, you might want to gather all these items before preparing the material.

Teaching/ Learning Strategies

The purpose of the teaching/learning strategies is to provide suggestions for introducing the materials. Some materials, especially many of the games, have specific strategies. Others can be placed in a classroom area for use during self-initiated or self-directed play.

Resources

Both your home and your community can be valuable sources for collecting recyclable free, or at least inexpensive, materials to work with. For example, such materials can be solicited from printing companies, grocery stores, junk yards, second-hand stores, pharmacies, fabric and craft stores, decorating stores, carpeting stores, office supply stores, restaurants, photography studios, hair stylists, bakeries, flower shops, gift shops, and card shops.
To assist you in the process of collecting recyclable materials, share the following list with your colleagues, parents, and classroom volunteers:

aluminum foil	beads
appliance boxes	braiding

buckles
buckram
burlap
buttons
calendars
canvas
cardboard sheets
cardboard tubes
carpeting
cellophane
ceramic tile
coffee cans
colored pictures
computer paper
confetti
cord
corrugated paper
drapes
egg cartons
felt
flannel
gloves
greeting cards
hardboard
hat boxes
jewelry
keys

magazines
measuring cups and spoons
newspapers
panty hose containers
paper bags
photographs
picture frames
plastic bags
plastic berry boxes
plastic bottles (detergent or
    deodorant)
plastic trays
plastic packing pieces
ribbon
rope
sandpaper
shoe boxes
spools
spray bottles
squeeze bottles
stamps
stationery boxes
thread
tongue depressors
wallpaper
wrapping paper

CONTENTS

ART   1

DRAMATIC PLAY   14

LANGUAGE ARTS   42

LARGE MOTOR   74

MATH   88

MUSIC   126

ROOM ENVIRONMENT   146

SCIENCE   182

SENSORY   232

SMALL MOTOR   248

SOCIAL STUDIES   266

WRITING CENTER   284

Designing Creative Materials For Young Children

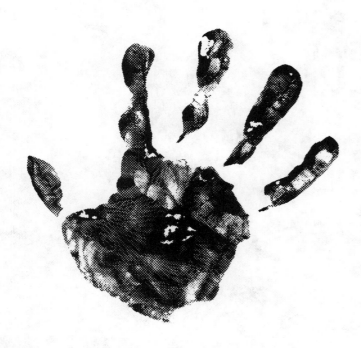

Chunk Crayons

| **Interest Areas** | art |
| | small motor |

| **Themes** | colors |
| | art |

Teacher Goals	faster color-recognition skills
	promote the development of small motor skills
	promote eye-hand coordination

Materials	small pieces of crayons
	muffin tin
	oven
	wax paper

Preparation

1. Turn the oven on and set it to 300°.
2. Place crayon pieces in the muffin tin.
3. Place the muffin tin in the oven, carefully monitoring the melting process.
4. Remove the warm, melted crayons from the muffin tin.
5. Cool until set and remove from tin.

Teaching/ Learning Strategies

Single-color or multicolored chunk crayons can be made. When making multicolored crayons, remove from the oven before they melt together and turn brown. Place the chunk crayons on the art table, easel, or in the art area. Provide paper for the children to scribble or draw on.

Crayon/Marker "Bundles" Chart

Crayon and Marker Bundles

To make a crayon or marker bundle you need:

crayon   or   marker

Wrap a few crayons or markers with a rubberband.

Color with the bundle to make a design.

Interest Areas

art
small motor

Themes

colors
art

Teacher Goals

encourage creative expression
promote experimentation with art media
promote the development of small motor skills
provide a stimulating environment
provide opportunities for following directions
encourage experimentation with cause-and-effect relationships

Materials

1 sheet of manila tagboard
colored felt-tip markers
clear contact paper or laminate

Preparation

1. On the tagboard, use the felt-tip markers to print the directions and draw the corresponding illustrations for making crayon or marker bundles (see photograph).

Crayon-and-Marker Bundles

a. To make a crayon or marker bundle you need:
crayons or markers
rubber bands
b. Wrap a few crayons or markers with a rubber band.
c. Color with the bundle to make a design.
2. Cover with clear contact paper or laminate.

Teaching/ Learning Strategies

Crayon/marker bundles are a wonderful addition to an art center. The bundles can be created by teachers or older children. They make unique and interesting designs. If desired, the art activity can be varied by making bundles of fewer or more crayons or markers and by changing the color combinations.

Colored-Sand Chart

Colored Sand

To make colored sand, mix together these ingredients.

sand

powder tempera paint

Squeeze glue onto paper and sprinkle the colored sand over the glue.

Interest Areas

art
language arts
science

Themes

sand and soil
art
colors

Teacher Goals

provide opportunities for following directions
promote experimentation with art media
promote the development of small motor skills
provide a variety of self-directed activities
create interest in the printed word

Materials

1 sheet of manila or white tagboard
colored felt-tip markers
clear contact paper or laminate

Preparation

1.   On the tagboard, use the felt-tip markers to print the directions and draw the corresponding illustrations for making colored sand (see photograph).

Colored Sand

a. Mix together 1 cup of sand and 1 tablespoon of powdered tempera paint.
b. Squeeze glue onto paper and sprinkle the colored sand over the glue.

2. Cover the chart with clear contact paper or laminate.

Teaching/ Learning Strategies

Gather the materials needed to make colored-sand designs and review the chart with the children. Encourage the children to help prepare the colored sand. For variety, mix several colors of sand. After sprinkling the colored sand on the glue, shake the piece of paper over a tray to remove the excess sand. Allow the designs to lay flat until dry.

Squeeze-Bottle Art Chart

Squeeze Bottle Art

For each color of squeeze bottle art mix these ingredients in a bowl.

or

Pour the mixture into a .

Squeeze the bottle onto paper or cardboard to create a design.

Interest Areas

art
small motor
science
math

Themes

art
colors
containers

Teacher Goals

promote the development of small motor skills
promote experimentation with art media
foster an awareness of changes in substances

Materials

1 sheet of manila tagboard
colored felt-tip markers
clear contact paper or laminate

Preparation

1. On the sheet of tagboard, use the felt-tip markers to print the recipe and draw the corresponding illustrations (see photograph).

   ### Squeeze-Bottle Art

   a. For each color of squeeze-bottle art, mix these ingredients in a bowl:
      1/2 cup water
      1/2 cup flour
      1/2 cup salt
      2 teaspoons powdered tempera paint or food coloring
   b. Pour the mixture into an empty, plastic squeeze bottle.
   c. Squeeze the bottle onto paper or cardboard, creating a design.
2. Cover the chart with contact paper or laminate.

Teaching/ Learning Strategies

Gather the materials and ingredients to prepare squeeze-bottle art and place the chart at the children's eye level. Encourage the children to help mix the paint. After the squeeze-bottle art is applied to construction paper or cardboard, allow the designs to lay flat on a surface until thoroughly dry. Younger children may also enjoy using the mixture for finger painting.

Deodorant-Bottle Painting

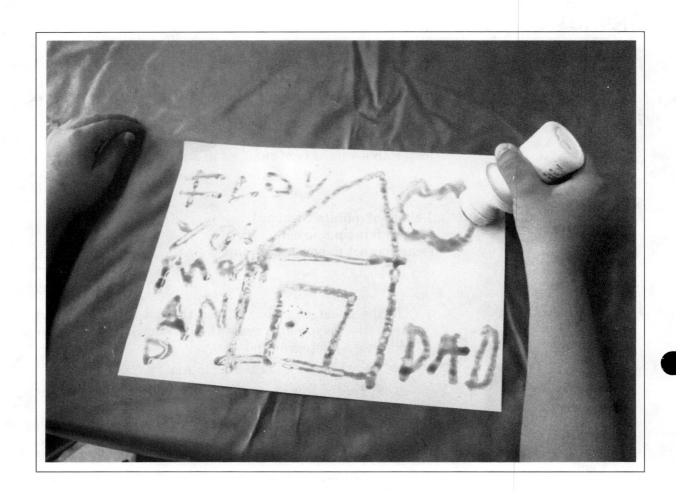

Interest Areas

art
small motor

Themes

colors
art

Teacher Goals

encourage experimentation with art media
promote the development of small motor skills
promote eye-hand coordination
encourage experimentation with cause-and-effect relation-
    ships
encourage creative expression

Materials

empty roll-on deodorant bottles
liquid starch
powdered tempera paint

Preparation

1. Carefully pry the ball out of a deodorant bottle and wash
    the inside of the container.
2. Fill the bottle three-quarters full of liquid starch and
    add 1/2 teaspoon of powdered tempera paint.
3. Securely place the ball back in the bottle and shake well.

Teaching/ Learning Strategies

The paint-filled deodorant bottles can be placed on the art
table and used with a variety of paper during self-directed
play periods. When the bottle is turned upside down and
rolled over the paper, it leaves a trail of paint. Prepare many
colors of paint to stimulate interest and encourage color
mixing.

Paint Pallets

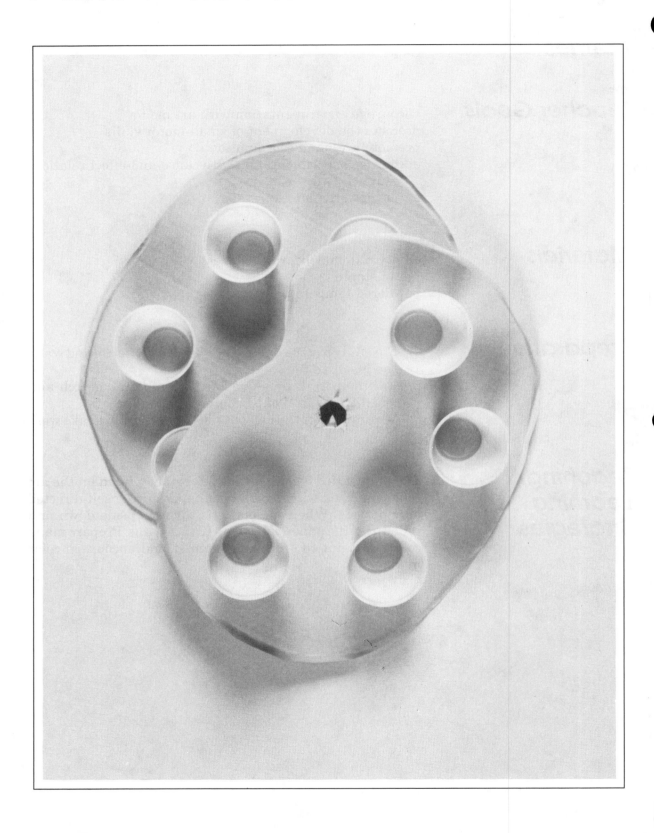

Interest Areas

art
dramatic play

Themes

art
occupations
colors

Teacher Goals

promote the development of small motor skills
promote eye-hand coordination
promote self-expression
reinforce color-recognition skills
promote esthetic appreciation

Materials

For each pallet:
1 piece of cardboard, 15 1/2" x 10"
colored contact paper
4 small plastic cups
scissors
hot glue gun, rubber cement, or glue

Preparation

1. Trace and cut a pallet pattern from a piece of cardboard (see photograph).
2. Cover the cardboard pallet with colored contact paper.
3. Cut a 1" hole to facilitate holding the pallet.
4. Attach the four small plastic cups to the pallet, using a hot glue gun, rubber cement, or glue.

Teaching/ Learning Strategies

Fill the small containers half full of a thick tempera paint. Place the paint pallets in the art area. The children will enjoy using them at the easel.

Dramatic Play

Bird Masks

Interest Areas

dramatic play
language arts

Themes

birds
masks
costumes
animals
acting

Teacher Goals

promote role-playing
stimulate language skills
encourage cooperation

Materials

1 sheet of tagboard
elastic
masking tape
stapler
craft knife
scissors
clear contact paper or laminate

Preparation

1. Trace a bird mask and beak pattern on tagboard.
2. Cut out the mask and beak.
3. Cut out two circles for eyes from the mask.
4. Cover the beak and mask with clear contact paper or laminate.
5. Using the craft knife, cut away the laminate from the eye holes.
6. Bend the beak in half and attach it to the inside of the mask, using a stapler.
7. Place masking tape around the staples to reinforce the beak.
8. Cut a piece of elastic long enough to fit around a child's head.
9. Staple the elastic to each side of the mask.

Teaching/ Learning Strategies

Place the bird masks where they are readily available, such as the dramatic-play area. A mirror may encourage play.

Bunny Ears

Interest Area	dramatic play
Themes	costumes rabbits/bunnies Easter animals
Teacher Goals	stimulate language skills foster creative expression promote role-playing
Materials	For each set of ears: white and pink fabric white thread needle scissors 1 piece of elastic, 12" long

Preparation

1. Cut two 3" x 6" pieces of white fabric in the shape of bunny ears. If desired, first construct a pattern out of paper.
2. Cut two 3" x 6" pieces of pink material to represent ears.
3. Sew the white and pink pieces together. The pink material will make up the front of the ears (see photograph).
4. Sew two 3" x 7 1/2" strips of white material on top of one another to make the base of the ears.
5. Sew the elastic and ears to the base.

Teaching/ Learning Strategies

Display bunny ears in the dramatic-play area or set them next to a mirror. The children will particularly enjoy the bunny ears around Easter or if a bunny has been added as a classroom pet.

Insect Costumes

| **Interest Areas** | dramatic play |
| | science |

Themes

insects
spring
costumes
acting

Teacher Goals

promote the development of large motor skills
promote role-playing
stimulate language skills

Materials

For each costume:
2 large, white sheets of tagboard
1 small plastic headband (can be purchased at a variety or
    department store)
2 black pipe cleaners
masking tape
felt-tip markers
scissors
2 pieces of elastic, 5" long

Preparation

1. Cut one large oval for a wing from each sheet of tagboard.
2. Decorate each oval, using felt-tip markers (see photograph).
3. Tape an elastic strip to each wing to slip over a child's arm.
4. Cover ovals with clear contact paper or laminate.
5. Bend two pipe cleaners around the headband, so they look like antennas, and curl the tops.

Teaching/ Learning Strategies

Insect costumes make interesting additions to the dramatic-play area and are especially useful for discussing related themes or seasons of the year.

Paper Bag Costumes

Interest Area	dramatic play

Themes

actors/actresses
occupations
Halloween
farm animals
fairy tales
communication
can be adapted to any theme

Teacher Goals

encourage creative expression
stimulate language skills
foster role-playing
promote social skills

Materials

For each costume:
1 large, paper grocery bag
scissors
colored, permanent felt-tip markers

Preparation

1. On the unmarked side of a paper bag, cut a circle large enough for a child's face.
2. Decorate the bag as desired, using felt-tip markers. For example, the bags can be decorated to represent people, animals, occupations, etc. (see photograph).

Teaching/ Learning Strategies

Adults or children can create paper bag costumes. For younger children, an adult will need to prepare the costume. Older children may enjoy creating their own. A series of costumes can be developed representing "Goldilocks and the Three Bears," "Little Red Riding Hood," "The Three Little Pigs," etc.

Clown Make Up

For each color mix:
3 to 5 drops
¼ c. cold cream

Apply to face with or a clean .

Interest Areas

dramatic play
art
science

Themes

circus
Halloween

Teacher Goals

provide materials to explore and learn about the environment
promote eye-hand coordination
promote color-identification skills
promote creative expression
foster an awareness of changes in substances

Materials

1 sheet of white tagboard
colored felt-tip markers
clear contact paper or laminate

Preparation

1. On the sheet of tagboard, use the felt-tip markers to print the recipe and draw the corresponding illustrations (see photograph).

   ### Clown Makeup

   a. For each color of makeup, mix these ingredients in a bowl:

   3 to 5 drops of food coloring
   1/4 cup cold cream

   b. Apply makeup by hand or with a clean paintbrush.
2. Cover the chart with clear contact paper or laminate.

Teaching/ Learning Strategies

Display the chart in the dramatic-play area directly above a table at the children's eye level. Place a large mirror on the table next to the chart so the children can watch themselves as they apply the makeup. Include this activity during self-directed play periods. The teacher should provide plenty of time for the children to experiment with the cause-and-effect relationship of preparing and applying the makeup. Young children learn by doing.

Yarn Wigs

| **Interest Areas** | dramatic play |
| | social studies |

Themes

hairstylist
occupations
colors
self-concept

Teacher Goals

encourage cooperation
promote role-playing
stimulate language skills

Materials

For each wig:
1 skein of rug yarn
scissors
ruler or tape measure

Preparation

1. Cut the skein of yarn into 2 feet or 3 feet lengths, depending on the length of wig desired.
2. Use one strand to represent the "part." Tie groups of three strands to the part at the center of each group. Proceed until all of the yarn is used. Tie off the part with a knot at each end.
3. Braid or style the wig as desired.

Teaching/ Learning Strategies

Use the yarn wigs in the dramatic-play area during self-directed play. To create interest, prop the wigs on empty plastic containers, such as detergent or 2-liter pop bottles. Call attention to the various colors, lengths, and styles of wigs. Add props, such as ribbons, bows, and barrettes, to extend the children's play.

Dance Tutus

Interest Areas

dramatic play
music
large motor

Themes

dance
movement
ballet
clothing
music

Teacher Goals

encourage creative expression
stimulate language skills
promote the development of large motor skills

Materials

For each tutu:
1 yard of colored netting
30" of ribbing
matching thread
needle
scissors
Velcro

Preparation

1. Cut colored netting into four strips, approximately 8" wide.
2. Gather and sew the four layers of netting to a 30" strip of ribbing.
3. Sew a 2" piece of Velcro on each end of the ribbing for use as a closure.

Teaching/ Learning Strategies

Place the tutus in either the dramatic-play or music area of the classroom. During self-directed play periods, the children can use the tutus for self-expression. Observe the children and, if needed, provide various musical backgrounds.

Car Wash

Interest Areas	dramatic play
	social studies
	small motor

Themes

transportation, cars, and trucks
water
wheels

Teacher Goals

encourage cooperation
introduce the uses of water
promote the development of small motor skills

Materials

1 cardboard box, approximately 11" x 14" x 10"
2 blue sheets of acetate or cellophane, 8" x 11"
cellophane or masking tape
white or tan contact paper
black felt-tip marker
scissors

Preparation

1. Use scissors to cut off the ends of the box, leaving approximately 1" around the edges.
2. Cover the box with white or tan contact paper.
3. Cut sheets of acetate in strips to cover the door (see photograph).
4. Tape the strips of acetate or cellophane to the inside of the open ends of the box.
5. Use a felt-tip marker to print the words "car wash" on the sides of the box or above the doors of the car wash.

Teaching/ Learning Strategies

Children can push small toy cars and trucks through the car wash. The activity can be extended by placing a shallow tray of water in the box to allow the children to wash the cars.

Gas Pump

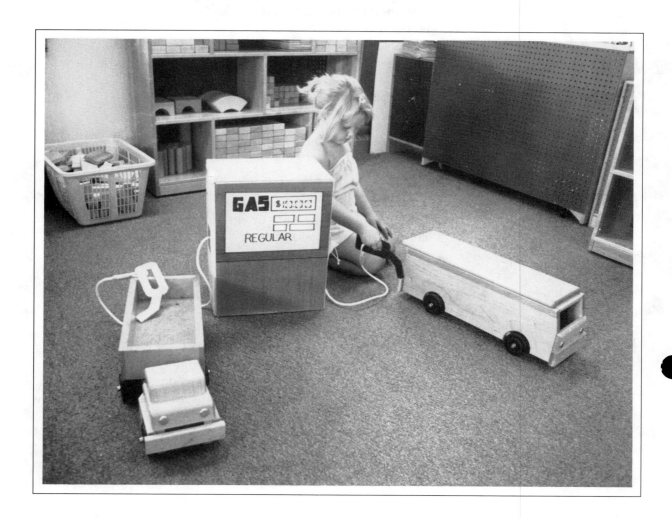

Interest Area	dramatic play

Themes
cars and trucks
transportation
auto mechanic

Teacher Goals
promote role-playing
encourage individual choices
stimulate language skills
promote social skills

Materials
1 14" x 18" box,
2 14" x 18" pieces of white construction paper,
2 3" x 8" pieces of construction paper,
2 pieces of yarn or rope, 24" long
contact paper
felt-tip markers

Preparation
1. Print the word "Regular" on one sheet of the white construction paper and "Unleaded" on the other (see photograph).
2. Glue the piece marked "Regular" to one side of the box and "Unleaded" to the other side.
3. Sketch and cut gas pump handles from the 3" x 8" pieces of construction paper.
4. Cut a small hole on each side of the gas pump for the handles.
5. Tie a knot at the end of each piece of rope.
6. Thread the ropes through the holes from inside the box until the knotted ends reach the holes.
7. Cover the handles with contact paper.
8. Attach rope or yarn to each handle.

Teaching/ Learning Strategies
Place the gas pump in the wheeled-toy area of the classroom or in the play yard. The children will enjoy "fueling" different types of transportation toys.

Interest Areas   dramatic play
language arts

Themes   letters
signs
can be adapted to any theme

Teacher Goals   promote letter-recognition skills
stimulate language skills
provide opportunities to decode symbols and written words
provide a print-rich environment
promote the development of language and literacy through
a meaningful experience

Materials   tagboard
scissors
stencils
pencil
glue or rubber cement
felt-tip markers

Preparation
1. Cut rectangles, approximately 14" x 24" from the tagboard.
2. Trace and cut letters for the signs—for example, Pet Store, Shoe Store, Paint Store.
3. Adhere the letters to the tagboard with glue or rubber cement.
4. Decorate the signs with related symbols.
5. Cover with clear contact paper or laminate.

Teaching/ Learning Strategies

Post the signs in the dramatic-play area. During group time, ask the children what addition has been made to the room.

Interest Areas	dramatic play social studies language arts
Themes	foods summer occupations numbers
Teacher Goals	promote role-playing encourage cooperation provide individual choices provide a print-rich environment reinforce left-to-right progression skills
Materials	1 sheet of white or manila tagboard black felt-tip marker construction paper scraps of brown, pink, green, white, and yellow rubber cement or glue scraps of burlap stapler

Preparation

To make the ice cream sign:
1. Print the words "Ice Cream" across the top of the tagboard sheet.
2. Draw and cut two ice cream cones from the brown construction paper. One cone will have a single scoop of ice cream, the other will have a double scoop (see photograph).
3. Adhere the ice cream cones to the sheet of tagboard with glue or rubber cement.
4. Print the words, "1 scoop—.35" and "2 scoops—.50" after the appropriate cone.
5. Cut out scoops of ice cream from the white, brown, pink, green, and yellow scraps of construction paper.
6. Glue the scoops to the bottom of the tagboard sheet and print the word "Flavors" above them.

To make ice cream cones:
1. Create a cone shape out of construction paper and staple or glue.
2. Cover the cone shape with burlap, using glue or rubber cement.
3. Trim the fabric.
4. Allow cones to dry before using.

Teaching/ Learning Strategies

Display the chart at the children's eye level in the dramatic-play area. Gather materials for an ice cream parlor, such as bowls, spoons, ice cream scoops, and empty, sterilized ice cream containers. Use styrofoam balls, pom-poms, or cotton balls to represent ice cream. Aprons and paper pads with pens or pencils may add interest to the activity.

Restaurant Menus

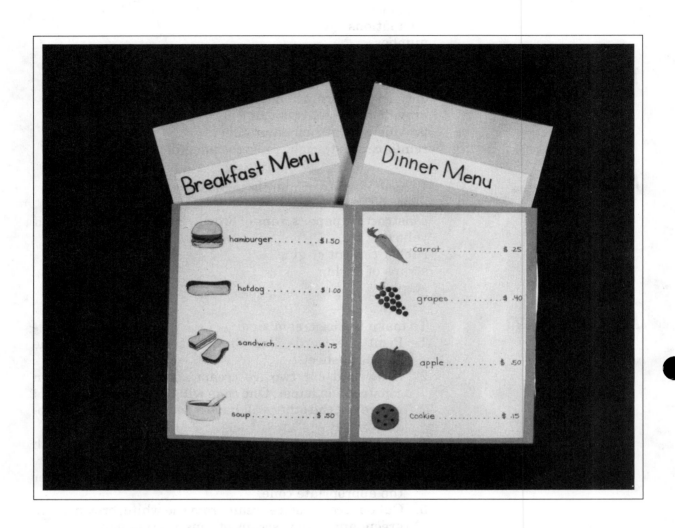

Interest Areas

dramatic play
language arts

Themes

restaurants
food
nutrition
occupations
community helpers

Teacher Goals

promote language skills
promote social skills
foster the identification of food products
promote number-identification skills
provide opportunities to decode symbols and written words
promote role-playing

Materials

For each menu:
1 sheet of construction paper, 12" x 18"
colored felt-tip markers
scissors
glue
pictures of food cut from magazines (optional)
clear contact paper or laminate

Preparation

1. Fold the construction paper in half.
2. Color small pictures of food or cut some out of magazines.
3. Glue the pictures of food onto the folded piece of construction paper.
4. Print the name of the food next to the picture.
5. Write the price of the food next to the crease in the paper.
6. Label the front of the menu.
7. Cover with clear contact paper or laminate.

Teaching/Learning Strategies

Arrange the dramatic-play area as a restaurant for the self-directed play period. Place the menus on the table and provide some pens and paper for the children to take orders. To extend this play, revise the menus to include symbols of money. For example, a quarter may be drawn next to the glass of milk.

Washing Machine and Dryer

| **Interest Areas** | dramatic play |
| | social studies |

Themes

clothes
water
laundromat

Teacher Goals

promote role-playing
encourage cooperation
foster an awareness of household tasks

Materials

2 cardboard boxes, approximately 12" x 15" x 20"
craft knife or scissors
spray paint or colored contact paper
construction paper scraps
glue or rubber cement

Preparation

1. Use a craft knife or scissors to cut a lid in the top of the box for the washing machine.
2. To make a dryer, cut an opening in the front of the other box.
3. Cover both boxes with colored contact paper or spray paint.
4. Cut circle shapes from construction paper scraps to represent buttons to operate the machines. Attach the shapes to the boxes with glue or rubber cement.

Teaching/ Learning Strategies

Place the washing machine and dryer in the dramatic-play area of the room. Additional props that may extend play include clothes, laundry baskets, empty detergent containers, a drying rack, and hangers.

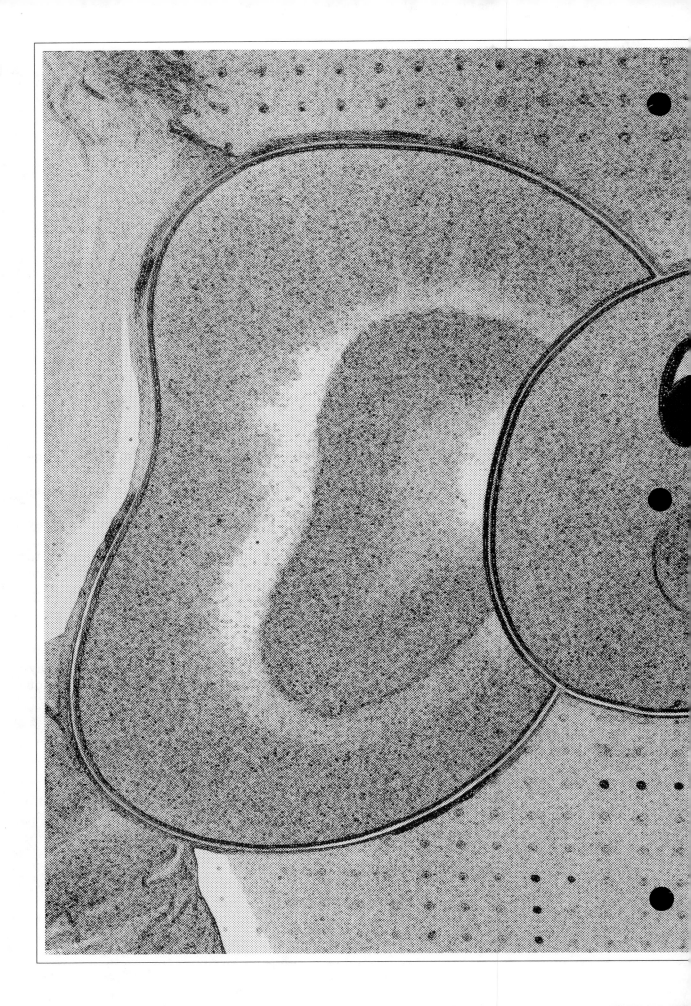

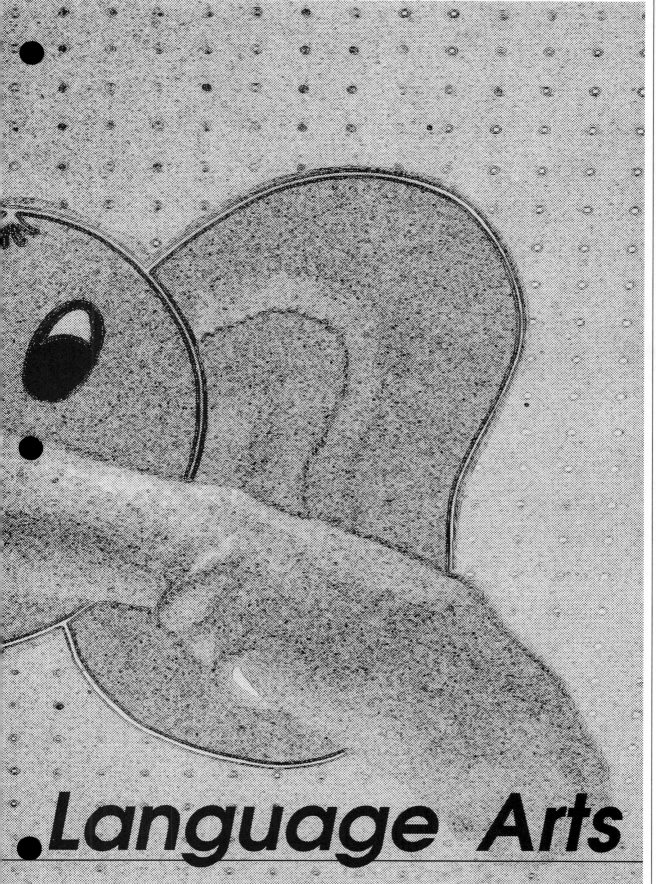

Language Arts

Egg-Carton Puppet

Interest Area

language arts

Themes

puppets
communication
feelings

Teacher Goals

encourage language skills
encourage creative expression
promote role-playing

Materials

1 egg carton
1 sock
scissors
contact paper scraps
craft pom-poms
movable plastic eyes (available at craft stores)
craft glue

Preparation

1. Use scissors to cut the egg carton in half.
2. Cut off the toe of a sock and glue the sock opening to the egg carton (see photograph).
3. Decorate the puppet as desired with contact paper scraps, pom-poms, and eyes.

Teaching/ Learning Strategies

Use the egg-carton puppet to tell stories or as a teaching aid. The puppet can also be placed in the language-arts area for use by the children. Extend this activity for older children by providing them with materials to make their own puppets.

Elephant Puppet

Interest Area	language arts

Themes	zoo
	circus
	animals
	wild animals

Teacher Goals	stimulate language skills
	encourage creative expression
	promote social skills
	promote eye-hand coordination
	encourage dramatization skills
	promote the development of large motor skills

Materials	1 piece of white tagboard
	oil-base crayons or colored felt-tip markers
	1 long gray sock
	scissors or craft knife
	pencil

Preparation

1. Trace the head and ears for an elephant and cut them out of the tagboard (see photograph).
2. Decorate the elephant, using gray, pink, and black oil-base crayons or colored markers.
3. Cut a circle in the tagboard for the elephant's nose.
4. Cover with clear contact paper or laminate.
5. Using the scissors or craft knife, cut away the clear contact paper or laminate from the circle.
6. Place the gray sock over your arm and insert it through the hole in the elephant.

Teaching/ Learning Strategies

During group time, encourage all children to pretend to be elephants. Ask questions, such as "How does an elephant move?" "How does an elephant eat?" "Where can we see elephants?" After the activity, place the puppet in the classroom so the children can learn through active exploration.

Glove Puppets

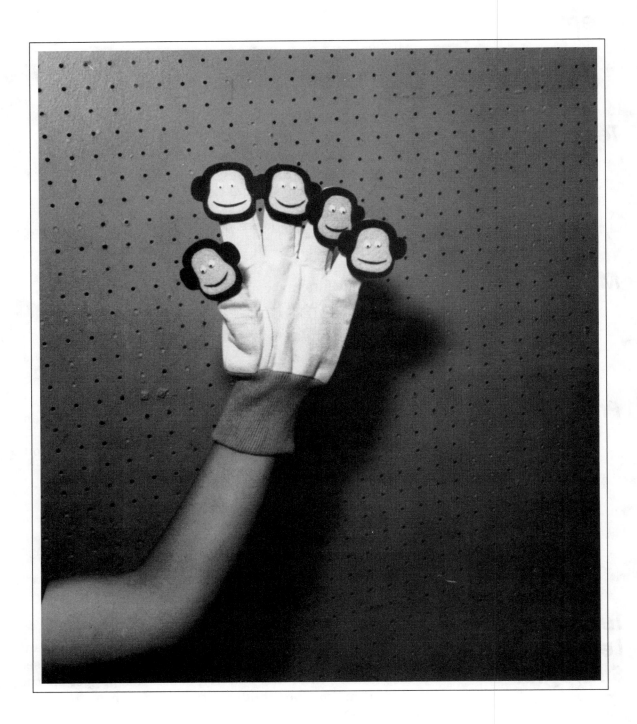

Interest Areas	language arts
	music

Themes

puppets
music
communication

Teacher Goals

stimulate language skills
promote the development of small motor skills
encourage creative expression

Materials

1 white garden glove
1 piece of Velcro, 5" long
glue, or needle and thread
felt
scissors
2 movable plastic eyes (available at craft stores)

Preparation

1. Cut a 1" piece of Velcro and glue or sew the loop side of the Velcro onto the bottom tip of each glove finger.
2. Construct felt figures that relate to a fingerplay that the children know. An example would be "Five Little Monkeys Jumping on the Bed."
3. Glue the corresponding 1" pieces of Velcro on the back of each felt figure.

Teaching/ Learning Strategies

To stimulate the children's interest, introduce the glove puppet during group time. It can also be used for story telling and fingerplays. Place the puppet in the room during free play for the children to spontaneously explore. They may enjoy repeating stories or creating their own.

Hamburger-Box Puppet

Interest Areas

language arts
dramatic play

Themes

puppets
communication
feelings

Teacher Goals

promote role-playing
stimulate language skills
promote the development of small motor skills
promote social skills
encourage creative expression
stimulate curiosity

Materials

1 Styrofoam hamburger box
contact paper
yarn
felt
glue
scissors
stapler
1 piece of elastic, 4" x 1"

Preparation

1. Disinfect the box with bleach if it has already had food in it.
2. Cover the top portion of the hamburger box with contact paper (see photograph).
3. Decorate the box as desired with the yarn and felt to represent a person or animal.
4. Staple a piece of elastic to the outside crease or spine of the box to make a handle for manipulating the puppet.

Teaching/ Learning Strategies

The puppet can be introduced by the teacher at group time. After this, place the puppet in the language-arts area or the dramatic-play area for the children's use during self-directed play. Extend this activity for older children by providing them with materials to make their own puppets.

Mouse Finger Puppet

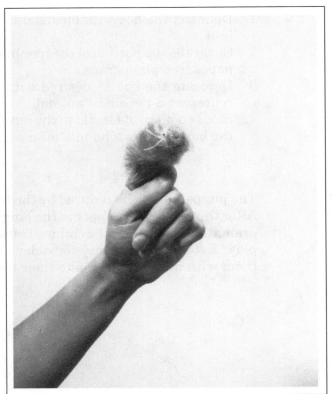

Interest Area

language arts

Themes

puppets
animals
communication

Teacher Goals

encourage creative expression
foster social skills
encourage dramatization skills
stimulate language skills
promote the expression of feelings
encourage individual choice

Materials

1 piece of gray, furry material
2 movable plastic eyes (available at craft stores)
tan felt
cream-colored thread
needle
scissors

Preparation

1. Sew up a 6" x 3" piece of furry material to fit over an index finger as a puppet.
2. Use thread to make the whiskers.
3. Attach movable eyes to the puppet face.
4. Cut and attach two 1/4" felt ears to the head of the puppet.

Teaching/ Learning Strategies

Use puppets for storytelling during group time. After this, place the puppet in the classroom for the children to spontaneously explore. The children can use the puppet individually or in small groups to tell familiar stories or create their own original stories during self-directed play periods.

Pop-Up Puppet

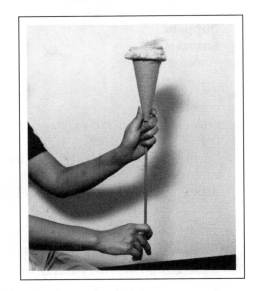

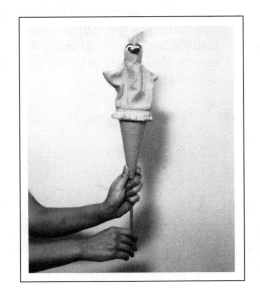

Interest Area	language arts
Themes	feelings puppets communication
Teacher Goals	stimulate language skills promote storytelling and role-playing facilitate social skills encourage individual choice
Materials	1 cardboard yarn cone 1 Styrofoam ball, 1" in diameter 1 wooden dowel, 1/4" in diameter, 18" long solid-color fabric yarn colored, permanent felt-tip markers construction paper scraps craft glue thread needle scissors
Preparation	1. Cover the yarn cone with fabric (see photographs). 2. Trace, cut, and sew the pattern for the puppet. 3. Insert the top of the dowel into the 1" Styrofoam ball. 4. Place the puppet over the Styrofoam, which will become the head. 5. Decorate the puppet with yarn, markers, and construction paper as desired. 6. Insert the dowel through the wide end of the yarn cone. 7. Glue the bottom edge of the puppet body to the wide opening of the yarn cone.
Teaching/ Learning Strategies	Use the puppet during storytelling and then place it in the language-arts area for use by the children during self-directed play periods.

Pot-Holder Puppets

| **Interest Areas** | language arts |
| | dramatic play |

Themes

animals
puppets
storytelling
can be adapted to any theme

Teacher Goals

stimulate language skills
promote storytelling and role-playing
encourage social skills
foster creative expression

Materials

For each puppet:
1 pot-holder
felt scraps
2 movable plastic eyes (available at craft stores)
scissors
craft glue or needle and thread
1 strip of elastic, 1" x 4"
protective fabric spray (optional)

Preparation

1. Decorate each pot-holder as desired, using the felt scraps and movable eyes (see photograph).
2. On the back of the pot-holder, glue or sew the strip of elastic. Sewing is usually more durable.
3. If desired, spray the puppet with protective fabric spray to keep it clean and prevent spotting.

Teaching/ Learning Strategies

Prepare pot-holder puppets to depict a favorite story, such as "The Three Little Pigs" or "Goldilocks and The Three Bears." To hold the puppet, the chid slips his or her hand under the elastic strip (see photograph). This activity can be extended by adding a puppet stage or theater to the classroom environment.

Magnetic Puppet Stage

Interest Areas	language arts
	dramatic play
	science

Themes

puppets
circuses
zoos
communication

Teacher Goals

stimulate language skills
promote the development of small motor skills
promote role-playing
foster eye-hand coordination
introduce science concepts through a meaningful experience

Materials

contact or wrapping paper
1 shoe box
tagboard
colored felt-tip markers
wooden dowels, 1/2" in diameter, 3" long
magnets
rubber cement
clear contact paper or laminate
story book or coloring book (optional)

Preparation

1. Cut out a rectangle from one side of the shoe box, leaving 1/2" edge along three sides (see photograph).
2. Cover the box with contact or wrapping paper.
3. Construct figures, using the tagboard and markers. They may relate to a favorite song or story. If desired, cut the figures from a storybook or coloring book. Cover the figures with contact paper or laminate. Glue tagboard to the back of each figure for reinforcement.
4. Cut a 1" x 1" square from the tagboard. Use the cardboard piece as a stand and glue it to each figure.
5. Attach a magnet to the top of each dowel and to the bottom of each figure stand, making sure that the corresponding magnetic poles attract.

Teaching/ Learning Strategies

Place the magnetic puppet stage in the dramatic-play, science, or language-arts area of the classroom. Encourage the children to move the figures by manipulating the dowel inserted through the opening. Older children may enjoy creating their own puppets and puppet stage.

Nylon Masks

Interest Areas

language arts
dramatic play

Themes

puppets
creativity
nursery rhymes

Teacher Goals

stimulate language skills
encourage creative expression
foster social skills
promote cooperation
encourage role-playing
promote an appreciation of storytelling

Materials

wire coat hangers
masking tape
nylons
scissor
glue
material scraps
pipe cleaners

Preparation

1. Bend the coat hanger to form a circle (see photograph).
2. Pull the nylon tightly over the coat hanger form. Wrap the nylon around the coat hanger and secure it with masking tape.
3. Decorate the puppet as desired with material and pipe cleaners to represent story characters, community helpers, or other people or animals.

Teaching/ Learning Strategies

Place the nylon masks in either the storytelling or language-arts area of the classroom. During self-directed play, the children can use the masks as puppets.

Aid for "Hickory Dickory Dock"

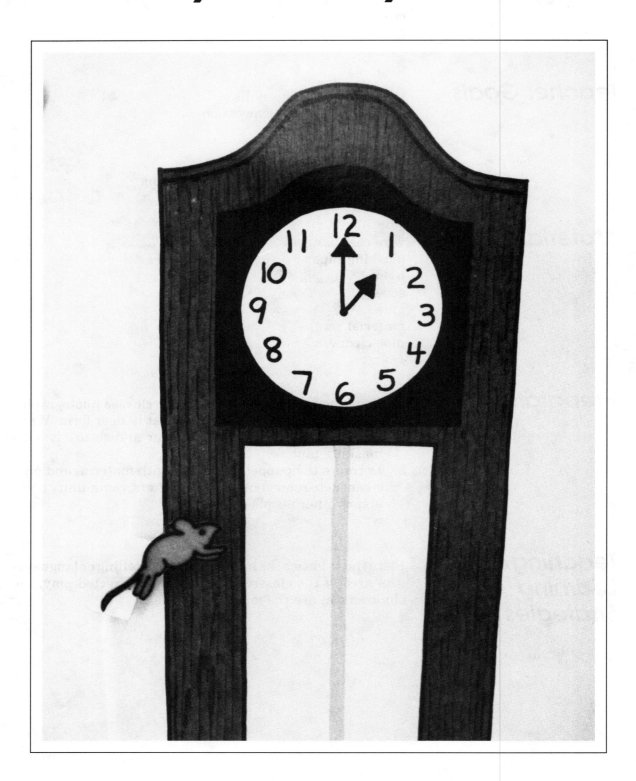

| **Interest Areas** | language arts |
| | music |

Themes
music/songs
time/measurement
animals
nursery rhymes

Teacher Goals
encourage the exploration of musical concepts
promote group cooperation
foster music appreciation

Materials
brown, black, and yellow felt-tip markers
1 piece of gray construction paper
1 piece of white yarn, 36" long
1 piece of white tagboard, 12" x 22"
paper punch tape
scissors
clear contact paper or laminate

Preparation
1. Use the felt-tip markers to draw a grandfather clock on the piece of tagboard (see photograph).
2. Punch two holes in the tagboard—one at the top and one at the bottom of the clock.
3. Draw and cut a mouse figure from the gray construction paper.
4. Cover the clock and mouse with clear contact paper or laminate.
5. Insert the yarn through the holes of the clock and tie as illustrated.
6. Attach the mouse to the yarn.

Teaching/ Learning Strategies
Use this aid as a motivational device during music time while singing, "Hickory Dickory Dock." The children might enjoy taking turns making the mouse move up and down the clock while singing.

Alphabet Book

Interest Area	language arts

Themes

books
letters
libraries
communication
sounds

Teacher Goals

promote letter-identification skills
encourage letter-object identification skills
promote the enjoyment of books
provide literacy concepts through meaningful experiences

Materials

27 pieces of tagboard, 11" x 8"
magazine, newspaper, and calendar pictures
several letters of different sizes cut from magazines, news-
    papers, and calendars
rubber cement
binder rings
paper punch
clear contact paper or laminate

Preparation

1. Cut letters and pictures from magazines, newspapers, and calendars for each alphabet letter.
2. Glue several, different-sized "A's" on the first page of the alphabet book.
3. On the opposite page, glue pictures of objects that begin with "A," such as apple, asparagus, and ape. Print the word of each object below its picture.
4. Continue this process, using a separate page for all letters of the alphabet.
5. Cover all pages with clear contact paper or laminate.
6. Punch two holes in the left side of each page.
7. Place rings in the holes of the pages to bind the book.

Teaching/ Learning Strategies

Attractively place the book in the reading corner. Encourage the children to look at the book. Ask if they can think of other objects that begin with each letter. This activity can be extended for older children. Provide magazines, newspapers, calendars, rubber cement, and tagboard or construction paper for them to make their own books.

"Peekaboo" Cards

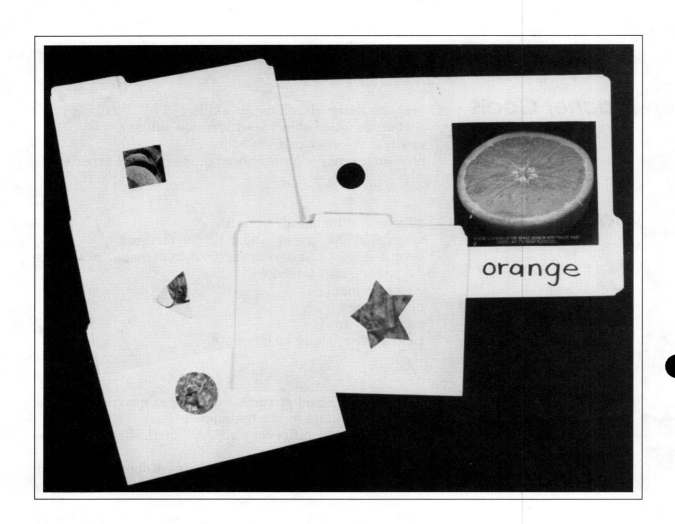

| **Interest Areas** | language arts |
| | reading readiness |

Themes

communication
feelings
self-expression
food
transportation
animals
games
sight

Teacher Goals

stimulate language skills
encourage prediction skills
foster visual-discrimination skills
encourage perseverance and task-completion skills

Materials

magazine pictures of familiar objects—animals, food, cloth-
    ing, transportation
manila folders
glue
scissors or craft knife
clear contact paper or laminate

Preparation

1. Cut pictures from magazines
2. Glue each picture inside a manila folder.
3. Using a craft knife, cut a small hole in the front of each
   folder, disclosing a small portion of the picture.
4. Open the folder and cover with clear contact paper or
   laminate.

**Teaching/
Learning
Strategies**

Place the peekaboo cards in the language-arts center. These
materials can be used individually or by small groups
during self-directed play periods. Show the children the
closed folder and demonstrate how to peek through the hole.
Then have the children describe the picture.

This activity can be adapted for 2- and 3-year-old children
by selecting pictures of a single, large, familiar object.
During preparation, cut a larger hole in the folder so it is
easier for them to identify the object.

Story Television Box

Interest Area	language arts
Themes	stories communication
Teacher Goals	promote an appreciation of storytelling promote listening skills foster object-identification skills
Materials	2 wooden dowels, 3/4" in diameter, 17" long 1 box, including lid, 16" x 9" scissors glue contact paper 2 identical storybooks (optional) roll of white shelf paper

Preparation

1. Cut a 10" x 13" hole in the lid of the box
2. Cut four 2" x 4" semicircles 1" from each corner of the box and four from the lid so that they line up with the holes in the box (see photograph).
3. Apply the contact paper to the box and lid. Trim the contact paper from the holes.
4. Cut pictures from the storybooks, using one book for the odd-numbered pages and the other for the even. If desired, the pictures can be drawn and filled in with crayon.
5. Glue the pictures on the roll of shelf paper. Provide enough space between pictures so only one will be displayed on the screen at a time.
6. Place the dowels in the semicircles in the box and attach each end of the paper story roll to the dowels.
7. Place the lid on the box, fitting the holes over the dowel ends.

Teaching/ Learning Strategies

The story television box can be used successfully at group time. Afterwards, place it in the language-arts center or storytelling area. The children can interact with it during self-directed play periods. Large amounts of uninterrupted time are needed for the children to enjoy this activity.

To encourage listening skills, the teacher can record the story on a cassette tape. An auditory signal, such as a played note, bell, or chime, can introduce each new page, cuing the children to turn the roll. Children can also be encouraged to experiment with language by inventing their own stories to go along with the pictures.

Rhyming Word Trains

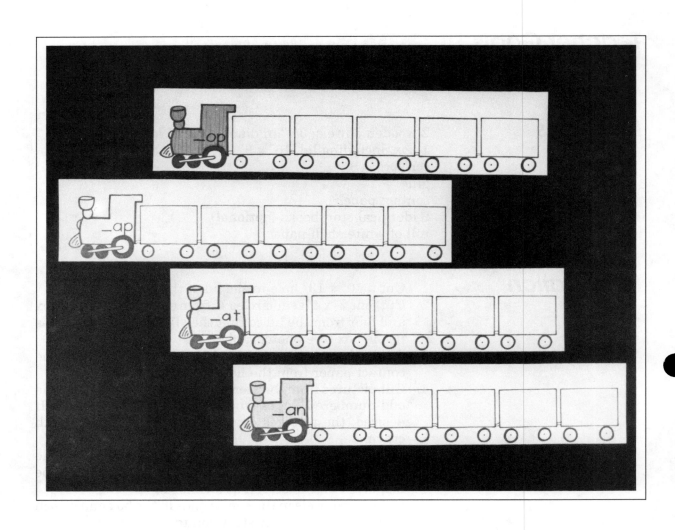

Interest Area	language arts
Themes	rhymes words sounds transportation
Teacher Goals	promote auditory-association skills encourage matching skills stimulate language skills promote group cooperation
Materials	5 pieces of white tagboard, 22" x 5" colored felt-tip markers 25 pieces of tagboard, 3" x 2" clear contact paper or laminate

Preparation

1. Draw and decorate a train engine and five accompanying white cars on each 22" x 5" piece of tagboard (see photograph).
2. On the first engine, draw a space and print the letters "__an."
3. On the second engine, draw a space and print the letters, "__ap."
4. On the third engine, draw a space and print the letters, "__op."
5. On the fourth engine, draw a space and print the letters, "__ot."
6. On the fifth engine, draw a space and print the letters, "__at."
7. On the 3" x 2" pieces of tagboard, print five rhyming words that correspond with each engine. For example, the words tan, ban, fan, man, and pan can be prepared for the first engine.
8. Cover all pieces with clear contact paper or laminate.

Teaching/ Learning Strategies

This activity is developmentally appropriate only for children who are beginning to decode the printed word. To encourage participation, place the trains in the language-arts area of the classroom. The children can sort through the set of 3" x 2" cards, placing the rhyming cards on the corresponding trains. The game can be played individually or in small groups of children. If and when necessary, demonstrate how to sort the cards.

Surprise Bags

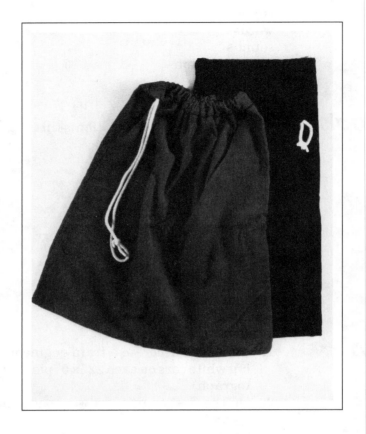

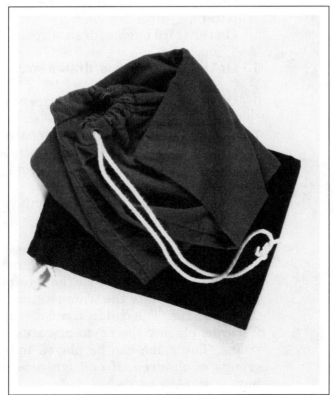

Interest Area	language arts

Themes

colors
can be adapted to any theme

Teacher Goals

promote object-identification skills
stimulate language skills
encourage prediction skills
stimulate curiosity

Materials

1 piece of bright, durable material, 40" x 45"
needle
thread
scissors
sewing machine
1 piece of rope or string, 45" long

Preparation

1. Fold the piece of fabric in half.
2. Sew two open sides closed.
3. Fold over the edge at the top and sew, creating a casing for the string.
4. Thread the string and tie the two ends together.

Teaching/ Learning Strategies

Store items used at group time in the surprise bags. Take one item at a time from the bag and introduce it to the children. Create interest by asking questions, such as "What do you think I have in my bag today?" Clues can be given—for example, "The item is red, a fruit, and grows on a tree." The bag can also be successfully used as a feely bag. Place an item in the bag and encourage the children to feel the bag, describe the object, and identify it.

Large Motor

Balloon Bats

Interest Area

large motor

● **Themes**

games
can be adapted to any theme

Teacher Goals

foster group cooperation
promote the development of large motor skills
promote eye-hand coordination
encourage individual choices

Materials

For each bat:
1 metal coat hanger
nylons
masking tape

Preparation

1. Bend the hanger to form a diamond or circle shape.
2. Twist the hook of the hanger to form a closed handle.
3. Place the nylon over the coat hanger form, securing it to the handle with masking tape.

● **Teaching/
Learning
Strategies**

Provide balloons. The bats and balloons can be used outdoors or indoors if sufficient space is available. For safety purposes, this activity needs to be carefully supervised. Balloons that burst should be immediately discarded by the teacher.

Movement Wands

| **Interest Areas** | large motor |
| | dramatic play |

Themes	creative movement
	feelings
	my body
	communication

Teacher Goals	promote the development of large motor skills
	promote creative expression
	encourage physical expression

Materials

For each movement wand:
1 wooden dowel, 1/2" in diameter, 12" long
acrylic paint
1 paint brush
1 screw eye, 1/4" in diameter
sandpaper
lengths of ribbon, yarn, or vinyl/plastic strips

Preparation

1. Sand the dowel, smoothing the ends and sides.
2. Paint the dowel and allow it to dry.
3. Insert a screw eye into one end of the dowel.
4. String lengths of ribbon, yarn, or plastic strips through the hole of the eye and secure with tape or by tying knots.

Teaching/ Learning Strategies

Place the movement wands in a large, open area indoors or outdoors. Encourage the children to move their wands and bodies freely. Extend this activity by playing records or a variety of musical instruments, such as the piano, drums, guitar, or rhythm instruments.

Creative Elastics

Interest Area	large motor
● *Themes*	my body exercise health shapes
Teacher Goals	promote the development of large motor skills foster problem-solving skills promote self-esteem
Materials	For each elastic: 1 piece of elastic, 1/2" wide, 65" long needle thread
Preparation	Using a needle and thread, securely sew the ends of the elastic together.
● *Teaching/ Learning Strategies*	Encourage the children to experiment with the creative elastics, allowing them to work independently or with others to explore the ways their bodies can move. Challenge older children to use their bodies with the creative elastic to form a specific shape or letter.

Dowel Horses

Interest Areas

large motor
dramatic play

Themes

horses/animals
farms
movement

Teacher Goals

promote the development of large motor skills
promote role-playing
foster cooperation and sharing

Materials

For each horse:
1 wooden dowel, 1" in diameter, 36" long
1/4 yard of fabric
2 craft animal eyes
yarn
stuffing (old nylons or polyester craft batting)
thread
needle
scissors
craft glue
sewing machine

Preparation

1. Cut two horse-head shapes out of the fabric (see photograph).
2. Use a sewing machine or needle and thread to sew the horse-head shapes together, leaving a 2" opening at the base of the neck.
3. Attach the craft animal eyes.
4. Stuff the horse head with discarded nylons or craft batting.
5. Place the horse head over one end of the dowel. Add more stuffing, if necessary.
6. Use a needle and thread to sew the opening closed.
7. For extra protection, apply craft glue to adhere the fabric to the dowel.
8. Sew or glue yarn to the horse head for a mane.
9. Tie yarn around the horse's mouth to represent reins.

Teaching/ Learning Strategies

Place the horses in an area with ample floor space. For safer use with younger or shorter children, cut off several inches from the dowels. To extend the activity, make a path or corral for the horses.

Footprints to Follow

Interest Area	large motor

Themes

body parts
travel
colors
movement

Teacher Goals

promote the development of large motor skills
promote visual-awareness skills
promote color-identification skills
encourage individual choice
encourage physical expression

Materials

colored construction paper
scissors
clear contact paper or laminate

Preparation

1. Trace and cut the form of a child's shoe onto colored construction paper. Repeat this process as many times as desired.
2. Cover footprints with clear contact paper or laminate.

Teaching/ Learning Strategies

This activity will encourage the children to be physically active. With the footprints, create an obstacle course indoors or outdoors for use during self-directed play periods. To extend the activity, the children can lay out the footprints, designing their own patterns. Also, teachers can arrange the footprints with other large-motor equipment, such as a tunnel, balance beam, and climber.

Hopscotch Mat

Interest Areas

large motor
math
social studies

Themes

my body
numbers
games
colors

Teacher Goals

promote the development of large motor skills
promote cooperation
introduce math concepts through a meaningful experience
review color concepts

Materials

1 sheet of clear plastic, 54" x 36"
contact-paper scraps
2 rolls of colored cloth tape, 3/4" wide
scissors
ruler

Preparation

1. Cut numbers out of the scraps of contact paper. The amount of numbers used will depend on the developmental level of the children.
2. Using the cloth tape and ruler, divide the plastic mat into 8" squares, creating a hopscotch board.
3. Center and adhere the contact-paper numbers in the squares (see photograph).

Teaching/ Learning Strategies

Place the hopscotch mat on the floor in the large-motor area with a beanbag. If desired, use the hopscotch board outdoors. Initially, the children may need assistance in playing the game. Demonstrate how to toss the beanbag.

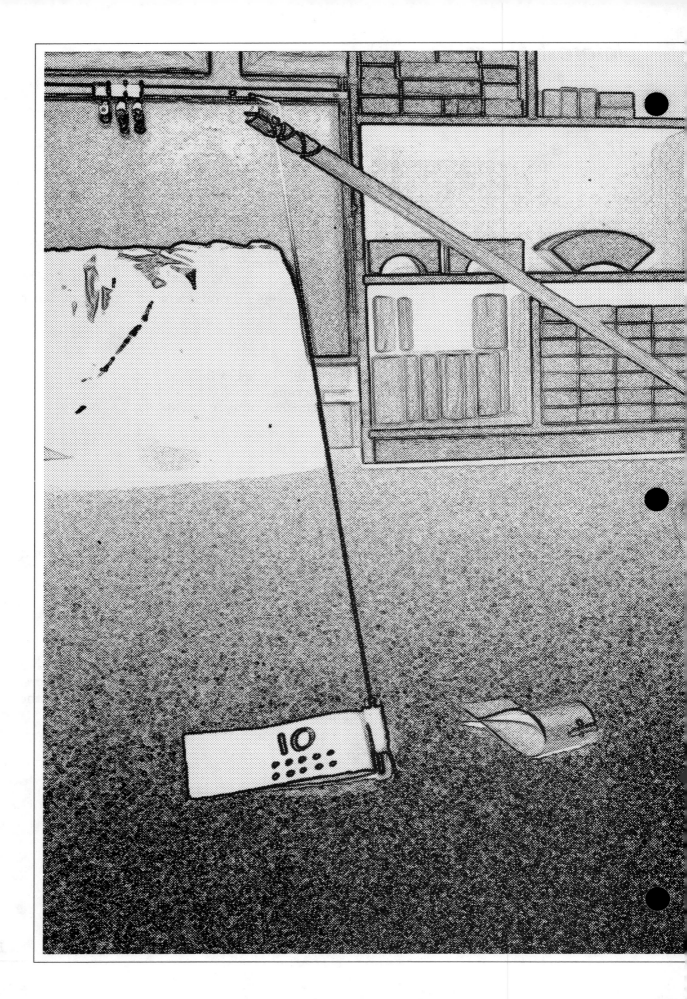

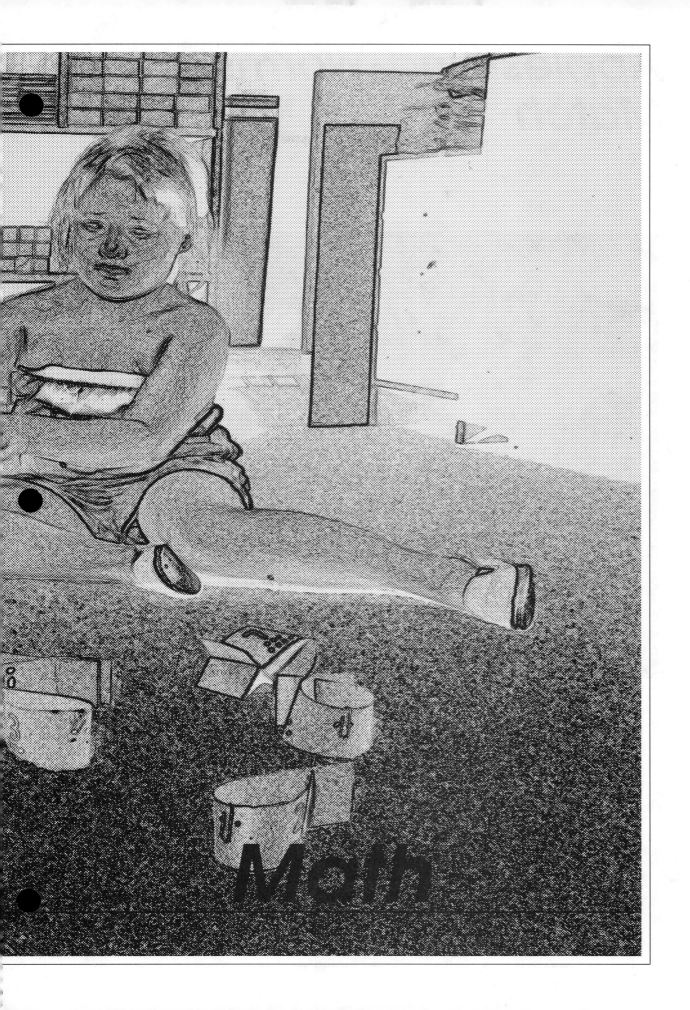

Apples-and-Worms Match

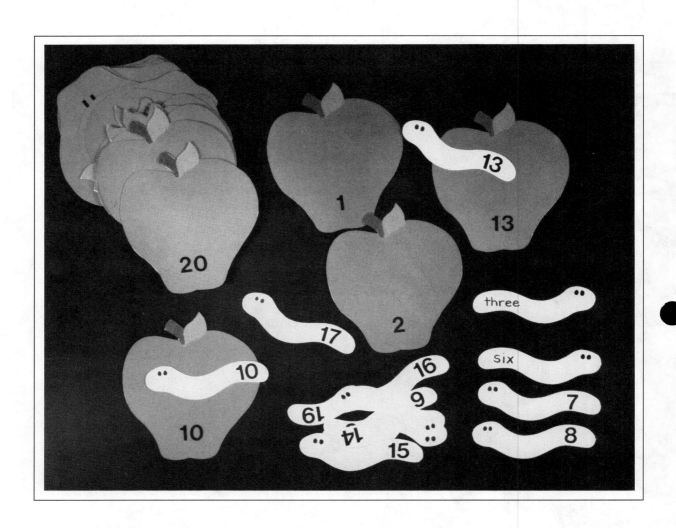

Interest Area   math

Themes
counting
food
fruits

Teacher Goals
promote matching skills
foster number-recognition skills
promote number correspondence

Materials
red, brown, green, white tagboard
black felt-tip marker
scissors
glue
clear contact paper or laminate

Preparation

1. Trace and cut 6" apples from the red tagboard.
2. Trace and cut 1" leaves from the green tagboard.
3. Attach a green leaf to each apple.
4. Trace and cut 1" stems from the brown tagboard.
5. Glue a stem to each apple.
6. Trace and cut 6" worms from white tagboard.
7. Trace and cut 2" worms from white tagboard.
8. Using a black felt-tip marker, print a number on each apple and on each 6" worm.
9. On the other side of the 6" worms, print the word of the corresponding number.
10. Add eyes to both sides of the 6" worms and the 2" worms.
11. Cover all pieces with clear contact paper or laminate.

Note: This activity and the following match games should be tailored to the children's developmental level. Teachers should prepare as few or as many counting materials to suit the abilities of the children. However, some teachers may elect to prepare additional materials for future use.

Teaching/ Learning Strategies

The object of this teacher-made game is to match the numbers on the worms with the corresponding numbers on the apples. Use the 2" worms to create sets to correspond with the numbers on the apples. This game can also be adapted as a bulletin-board activity.

Apple-Trees Flannel Board Match

Interest Area	math

Themes

counting
food
fruits
fall

Teacher Goals

promote counting skills
encourage number-recognition skills
foster visual-discrimination skills
promote the development of small motor skills

Materials

4 pieces of green felt, 8" x 11"
2 pieces of brown felt, 8" x 11"
2 pieces of red felt, 8" x 11"
scissors
hot-glue gun or craft glue

Preparation

1. Trace and cut green treetops and brown tree trunks. The number prepared should depend on the developmental level of the children.
2. Using a hot-glue gun or craft glue, adhere the treetop to the tree trunk.
3. Trace and cut 1" red apples and 1/4" brown stems.
4. Glue the stems onto the apples.
5. Trace and cut numbers out of the red felt.
6. Attach one number to each tree trunk.
7. Cut 1/4" red squares and attach the appropriate number of squares to the corresponding tree trunk (see photograph).

Teaching/ Learning Strategies

Place the materials in the appropriate area of the classroom for use during self-directed play periods. The children use the materials by counting the apples and placing the correct number on the corresponding treetops. Children may elect to participate individually or in small groups.

Baseball-and-Glove Match

Interest Area	math
● *Themes*	balls summer sports gloves
Teacher Goals	encourage number-recognition skills foster eye-hand coordination encourage social skills
Materials	2 sheets of brown tagboard 1 sheet of white tagboard paper punch glue black felt-tip marker scissors clear contact paper or laminate

● *Preparation*

1. Trace and cut baseball gloves out of the brown sheet of tagboard. The number prepared should depend on the developmental level of the children.
2. Trace and cut the same number of baseballs out of the white sheet of tagboard (see photograph).
3. Print a different number on each baseball.
4. Create white dots, using a paper punch.
5. Glue a different number of dots to each baseball glove.
6. Cover all pieces with clear contact paper or laminate.

Teaching/ Learning Strategies

Place the activity in the small-motor area of the classroom for use during self-directed play periods. Children may want to participate individually or in small groups. The purpose of the game is to match the printed number on the baseball with the number of dots on the corresponding baseball glove.

Football-and-Clothespin Match

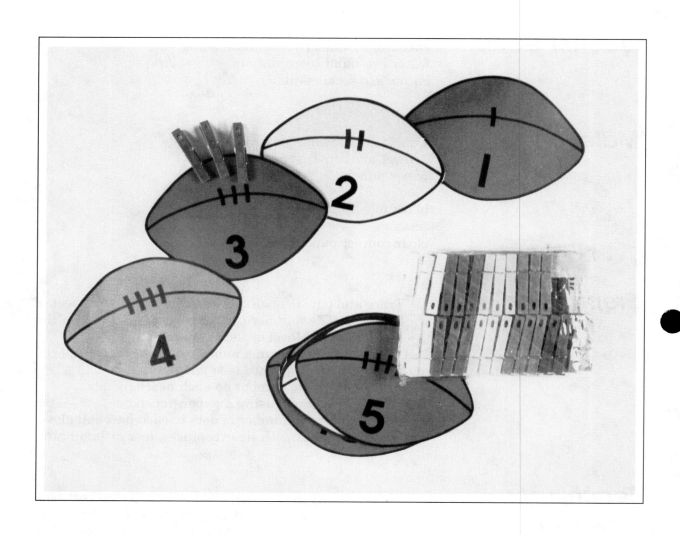

Interest Areas

math
small motor

Themes

sports
fall
fasteners
colors
balls

Teacher Goals

promote the development of small motor skills
encourage number-recognition skills
improve counting skills
promote eye-hand coordination
introduce math concepts through a meaningful experience

Materials

1 sheet of brown tagboard
black felt-tip marker
scissors
clothespins
clear contact paper or laminate

Preparation

1. Trace and cut a set of footballs out of tagboard. The number prepared should depend on the developmental level of the children.
2. Print a number on each football.
3. Use the black felt-tip marker to draw a set of stitches on the football to correspond with the printed number.
4. Cover all pieces with contact paper or laminate.

Teaching/ Learning Strategies

Place a box of clothespins next to the footballs for use during the self-directed play period. The object is to have the children attach the same number of clothespins to the football as the printed number or number of stitches. If needed, demonstrate how to attach the clothespins to the football.

Ice-Cream Cone Match

Interest Area	math

Themes
    summer fun
    food

Teacher Goals
    encourage visual-discrimination skills
    encourage number-recognition skills
    promote number correspondence
    facilitate matching numbers to sets

Materials
    brown, green, pink, and white tagboard
    colored construction paper
    paper punch
    scissors
    glue or rubber cement
    clear contact paper or laminate
    black felt-tip marker

Preparation

1. Trace and cut ice-cream cones from brown tagboard. The number prepared should depend on the developmental level of the children.
2. Trace and cut ice-cream scoops from pink, green, and white tagboard.
3. Use the paper punch to make dots out of construction paper.
4. Glue varying numbers of dots onto the ice-cream scoops.
5. Print a number on the ice-cream cone that corresponds with the number of dots on the ice-cream scoop.
6. On the back of the ice-cream scoop, print the number that corresponds to the amount of dots on the other side, so the game is self-correcting.
7. Cover all pieces with clear contact paper or laminate.

Teaching/ Learning Strategies

Children can participate in this activity individually or in small informal groups during the self-directed play period. The objective of the game is to match the ice-cream scoop with the corresponding cone.

Plastic-Eggs-and-Pom-Poms Match

| Interest Areas | math |
| | small motor |

Themes

numbers
farm animals
Easter

Teacher Goals

promote the development of small motor skills
encourage eye-hand coordination
foster number-recognition skills
promote color-recognition skills

Materials

12 plastic, colored eggs (can be purchased at a variety store)
1 egg carton
pom-poms of various colors (can be purchased at a craft or
    fabric store)
plastic rub-on numbers or black, permanent felt-tip marker

Preparation

Print or apply different numbers on each egg, beginning with 1. The number prepared should depend on the developmental level of the children.

Teaching/ Learning Strategies

Place this activity in the math-learning center or small-motor center. It should be provided as a self-directed activity, which, if needed, is teacher supported. Place the pom-poms in a small basket. Then encourage the children to look at the printed number on each egg and fill it with the corresponding number of pom-poms.

Snowpeople-and-Hats Match

Interest Area	math

Themes

games
numbers
winter

Teacher Goals

promote visual-perception skills
promote one-to-one correspondence
foster number-recognition skills
foster matching skills

Materials

white and blue tagboard
black, red, pink, and blue construction paper
paper punch
glue
black felt-tip marker
clear contact paper or laminate

Preparation

1. Trace and cut out snowpeople. The number prepared should depend on the developmental level of the children.
2. Trace and cut hats for each snowperson.
3. Punch dots out of the construction paper.
4. On one side of the hat print a number and on the other side glue the corresponding number of dots.
5. On the snowpeople, glue dots corresponding to the number of dots on the hat.
6. Glue eyes, a nose, and a mouth made from construction paper on each snowperson.
7. Cover all pieces with clear contact paper or laminate.

Teaching/ Learning Strategies

This activity can be used successfully during self-directed play periods. The children match the hats with the corresponding snowpeople. The adult can guide the children to match the dots on the hats with the corresponding dots on the snowpeople or to match the numbers on the other side of the hats with the corresponding number of dots on the snowpeople.

Watermelon-and-Plate Matching

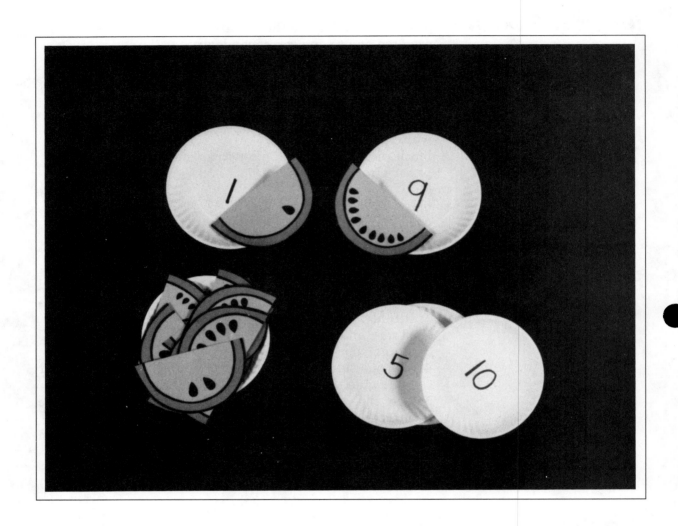

Interest Areas

math
small motor

Themes

fruits
foods
summer
seeds

Teacher Goals

promote one-to-one correspondence
facilitate number-identification skills
promote the development of small motor skills

Materials

green and pink construction paper
small paper plates
black felt-tip marker
scissors
glue or rubber cement
clear contact paper or laminate

Preparation

1. Cut watermelon slices from green and pink construction paper (see photograph). The number prepared will depend on the developmental level of the children.
2. Draw varying numbers of seeds on the front of each slice of watermelon.
3. Print the corresponding number and word on the back of each watermelon slice, as well as on a paper plate.
4. Cover the watermelon slices with clear contact paper or laminate.

Teaching/ Learning Strategies

Place the watermelons and plates in the math-learning or small-motor area. Initially, children may need to be shown how to match the slice of watermelon to the corresponding plate.

Dog-and-Bone
Folder Game

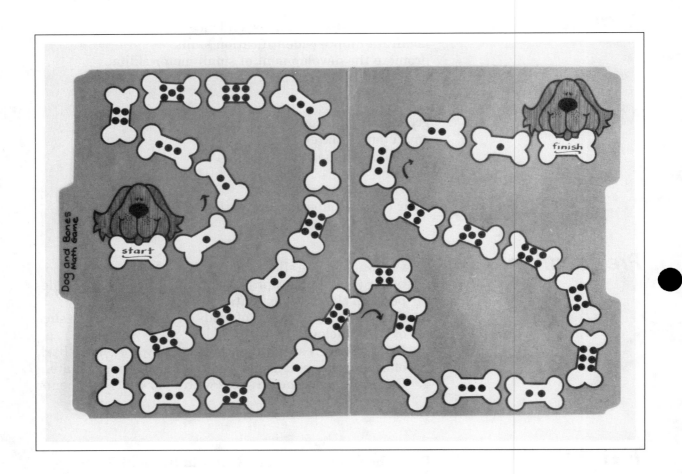

| **Interest Areas** | math |
| | small motor |

Themes	animals
	pets
	dogs
	bones

Teacher Goals

encourage group cooperation
foster visual-discrimination skills
promote the development of small motor skills
encourage eye-hand coordination
provide opportunities for following directions

Materials

1 blue file folder or sheet of blue construction paper
white and black construction paper
paper punch
glue
brown, red, and black felt-tip markers
scissors
clear contact paper or laminate

Preparation

1. Cut and glue 2"white bones in a game-board format on the folder (see photograph).
2. Prepare black circles, using a paper punch.
3. Glue the black circles onto the bones, six being the highest number. The bones can be placed on the game board sequentially (for example, 1–6) with the sequence repeated several times, or they can be placed randomly (for example, 2, 6, 4, 3, 1, 5, 6, 2, 1, etc.).
4. Trace and cut two dogs with a bone in their mouth.
5. Decorate the dogs using felt-tip markers.
6. Print the word "Start" on one dog and "Finish" on the other.
7. Glue the "Start" dog to the appropriate place on the folder. Do the same with the "Finish" dog.
8. Cut four round circles from construction paper scraps to be used as board markers.
9. Cover all pieces with clear contact paper or laminate.

Teaching/ Learning Strategies

The children play this game by shaking a die and moving their markers to the bone that corresponds to the number of circles on the die. The game ends when a marker lands next to or closest to the finish. Usually, this game is best played in small groups or with a teacher and child.

Halloween Ghosts
Folder Game

Interest Area	math

Themes

Halloween
numbers
games

Teacher Goals

introduce math concepts through meaningful experience
promote an awareness of sets
foster group cooperation
encourage independence

Materials

1 orange file folder or sheet of orange construction paper
2 sheets of white construction paper
orange construction paper scraps
colored felt-tip markers
glue or rubber cement
paper punch
scissors
clear contact paper or laminate

Preparation

1. Draw and cut out approximately 30 ghosts, 1/2" x 1", from the white construction paper.
2. Use a paper punch to make small orange circles. Glue the circles onto the ghosts, six being the highest number.
3. Glue the ghosts to an open file folder sequentially (1–6, repeated several times) or randomly (2, 5, 3, 4, 6, 1, 3, 4, 6, etc.).
4. With a felt-tip marker, print "Start" and "Finish" on separate ghost pieces and glue each piece in the appropriate place on the folder.
5. Cut four round circles from construction paper scraps to be used as board markers.
6. Laminate all pieces.

Teaching/ Learning Strategies

Provide a die and give each player a marker. The children take turns rolling the die, and moving their markers to the nearest ghost with the corresponding set of dots. The game ends when a marker lands next to or closest to the finish. For older children, extend this activity by making a spinner with numbers.

Valentine Folder Game

Interest Area Themes

math

Valentine's day
games
paper
holidays
can be adapted to any theme

Teacher Goals

encourage group cooperation
provide opportunities for following directions
promote counting skills
foster visual-discrimination skills
promote the development of small motor skills
encourage eye-hand coordination

Materials

1 red file folder or large sheet of red construction paper
white, pink, red, and black construction paper
pink tagboard
glue
scissors
black felt-tip marker
paper punch
1 brass fastener
clear contact paper or laminate

Preparation

1. Cut and glue 1" white hearts in a game-board format onto the file folder (see photograph).
2. Glue a 2" pink heart onto a 3" red heart, creating a pink-and-red heart. Repeat this process once.
3. Print the word "Start" on one pink-and-red heart and "Finish" on another and glue each piece in the appropriate place on the folder.
4. Punch red dots out of red construction paper.
5. Glue the red dots to the 1" white hearts, varying the number of circles on the hearts. The dots can be placed sequentially (1–6 repeated several times) or randomly (5, 3, 1, 2, 4, 6, 3, 6, 2, etc.).
6. Cut a 6" circle from the pink tagboard to use as a spinner.
7. Divide the circle into six equal sections, using the black marker.
8. Glue a 1" white heart onto each section.
9. Glue red dots onto each white heart from 1–6.
10. Cut four round circles from construction paper scraps to be used as board markers.
11. Cover all pieces with clear contact paper or laminate.
12. Cut a 2" black arrow from construction paper.
13. Use a brass fastener to attach the arrow to the middle of the spinner.

Teaching/ Learning Strategies

The children play this game by twirling the spinner, looking at the number, and moving their markers to the corresponding heart on the folder. The game ends when a marker lands next to or closest to the finish. Some children may need assistance with this activity. Use fewer dots on the hearts for younger children.

Floor Shape Puzzle

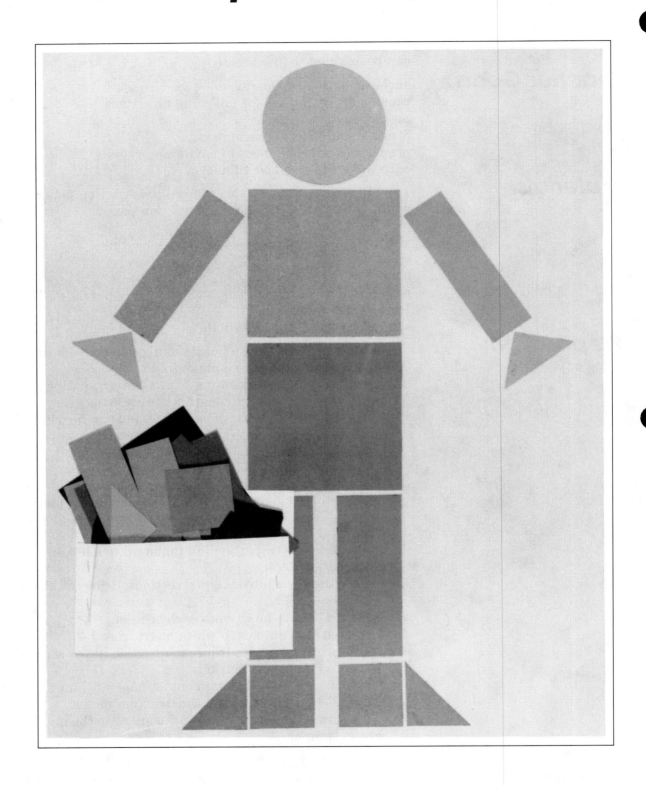

Interest Area

math

● Themes

shapes
colors
puzzles

Teacher Goals

foster eye-hand coordination
promote the development of small motor skills
foster shape-identification skills
promote color-identification skills
foster problem-solving skills

Materials

1 piece of tagboard
colored construction paper
rubber cement or glue
clear contact paper or laminate

Preparation

1. Cut shapes—circles, squares, rectangles, and triangles—
   from construction paper. Make two identical shapes:
   one to glue to the tagboard and the other for the children
   to match.
2. Arrange the shape pieces on the tagboard to form a
   picture and glue.
3. Cover the tagboard and all pieces with clear contact
   paper or laminate.

Teaching/ Learning Strategies

The purpose of this puzzle is to have the children match the
loose shapes with the corresponding shapes on the tagboard.
Design the puzzle to suit the children's developmental level.
For younger children, the two corresponding shapes can be
the same color. To make the puzzle more challenging for
older children, cut all of the loose shapes out of the same
color and vary the color of the shapes in the puzzle.

Valentine Heart Puzzles

Interest Areas	math small motor

Themes   Valentine's Day

Teacher Goals

encourage counting skills
stimulate number-recognition skills
promote one-to-one correspondence
foster visual-discrimination skills

Materials

pink or red tagboard
white construction paper
black felt-tip marker
scissors
glue
clear contact paper or laminate

Preparation

1. Cut 5" hearts out of the tagboard.
2. Cut each heart into two puzzle-shaped pieces (zigzag, wavy, straight edge).
3. On one half of the heart, glue a small 1" heart cut from construction paper. On the other side of this half, print the number "1" and the word "one."
4. On the other half of the heart, print the number "1" and the word "one."
5. Repeat this process for the numbers 2–10 or until you have prepared an amount suited to the developmental level of the children.
6. Cover all pieces with clear contact paper or laminate.

Teaching/ Learning Strategies

The children should match the halves of the hearts and then sequence the numbers from 1–10.

Favorite-Colors Chart

name	red	yellow	blue	orange	green	purple	pink	brown	white	black	other	
How many people liked the same color?												

Our Favorite Colors

Interest Areas

math
language arts

Themes

colors
counting
I'm special

Teacher Goals

promote color awareness
encourage color-identification skills
foster counting skills
promote the development of language and literacy through
    a meaningful experience
promote self-esteem
create a print-rich environment

Materials

1 sheet of tagboard
black felt-tip marker
colored construction paper
ruler
clear contact paper or laminate

Preparation

1. Print the words "Our Favorite Colors" across the top of
   the tagboard (see photograph).
2. Below the title, print the word "Name" and each color
   included on the chart.
3. Place a 2" x 1" corresponding-color piece of construction
   paper, below each color name.
4. Using a ruler, make vertical and horizontal lines on the
   chart.
5. Leave spaces to print each child's name along the
   vertical edge of the tagboard.
6. On the last line, print the words "How many people liked
   the same color?"
7. Cover with clear contact paper or laminate.

**Teaching/
Learning
Strategies**

This chart can be used during group time to identify colors
and practice counting. This activity teaches children that
people have different color preferences. After group time,
hang the chart in the classroom as a communication to
visitors and a contribution to a print-rich environment.

Favorite-Fruits Graph

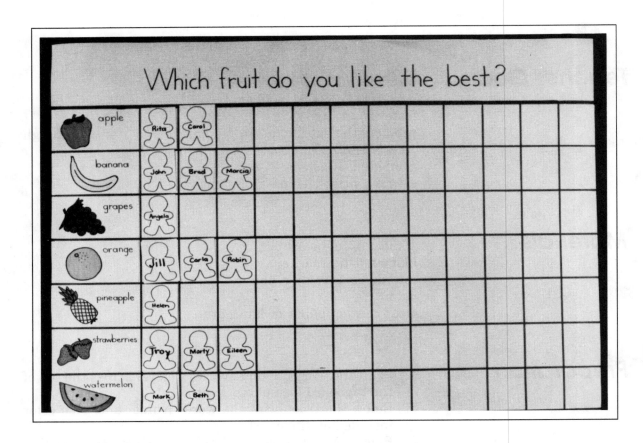

Which fruit do you like the best?

	apple	Rita	Carol								
banana		John	Brad	Marcia							
grapes		Angela									
orange		Jill	Carla	Robin							
pineapple		Helen									
strawberries		Troy	Marty	Eileen							
watermelon		Mark	Beth								

Interest Areas

math
language arts

Themes

food
fruits
counting

Teacher Goals

promote fruit identification skills
provide a print-rich environment
foster name-recognition skills

Materials

1 or 2 sheets of tagboard
colored felt-tip markers
1 piece of tagboard for each child, 2 1/2" x 3"
clear contact paper or laminate

Preparation

1. Across the top of the tagboard, print the words "Which fruit do you like best?"
2. From top to bottom, on the left side of the tagboard, draw pictures of common fruits. Print the name beside each fruit (see photograph).
3. On each 2 1/2" x 3" piece of tagboard, make a gingerbread pattern.
4. Print each child's name inside the pattern.
5. Cover all pieces with clear contact paper or laminate.

Teaching/ Learning Strategies

Schedule this activity during group time. Taking turns, ask each child to name a favorite fruit. Then give the child his or her name tag to place on the chart behind the appropriate fruit. Once everyone has had a turn, count how many children like apples, oranges, pineapples, etc. After group time, hang the chart in the classroom.

Favorite-Vegetables Chart

Interest Areas

math
language arts

Themes

foods/vegetables
gardens
plants
self-concept

Teacher Goals

encourage group participation
foster an appreciation for individual differences
introduce math concepts through a meaningful experience
promote classification skills
provide a print-rich environment

Materials

1 sheet of tagboard
colored felt-tip markers
clear contact paper or laminate

Preparation

1. Using a black felt-tip marker, print the following captions on the tagboard sheets:

   We like corn.
   We like peas.
   We like carrots.
   We like potatoes.
   We like beans.

2. Illustrate each vegetable listed on the tagboard and color with felt-tip markers (see photograph).
3. Cover the chart with clear contact paper or laminate.

Teaching/Learning Strategies

During group time or self-directed play periods, ask each child to select a favorite vegetable and print his or her name on the chart underneath the appropriate vegetable with a watercolor marker. Older children may enjoy printing their own names. After all the children have participated, determine how many children like each vegetable, which vegetable is most popular, which vegetable is least favorite, etc. Hang the chart in the room at the children's eye level.

"How Did You Come to School?" Chart

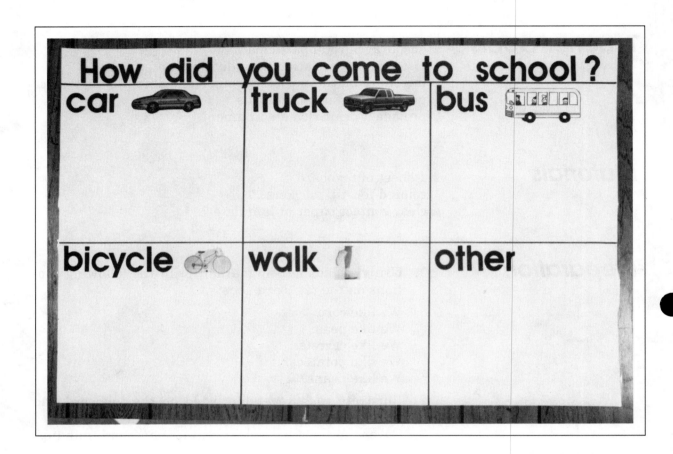

Interest Areas

math
social studies

Themes

transportation
trucks and cars
wheels

Teacher Goals

introduce types of transportation
promote name-recognition skills
introduce math concepts through a meaningful experience

Materials

1 piece of tagboard
magazine pictures of a car, truck, bicycle, and a person
    walking (optional)
glue
black felt-tip marker
clear contact paper or laminate
ruler

Preparation

1. Print the words "How did you come to school?" across the top of the tagboard (see photograph).
2. Divide the rest of the tagboard into six equal parts, using a ruler and a marker.
3. In each space, print the word of a different type of transportation—car, truck, subway, bus, bicycle, etc.
4. In each space, draw or glue a picture next to the corresponding word.
5. Cover the chart with clear contact paper or laminate.

Teaching/ Learning Strategies

During group time, ask each child how he or she came to school. Using a watercolor marker, print the child's name in the appropriate space on the chart. After everyone has had a turn, encourage the children to count how many came in a car, truck, bus, etc. After recording these numbers, determine if more children rode in a truck than a car, than a bus, etc.

Fishing Fun

Interest Area	math

Themes

water
pond life
occupations
hobbies

Teacher Goals

promote number-recognition skills
foster counting skills
encourage group cooperation

Materials

10 strips of construction paper, 12" x 2"
black felt-tip marker
10 paper clips
1 wooden dowel, 1/2" in diameter, 15" long
1 small magnet
string
scissors
clear contact paper or laminate

Preparation

1. Print the number "1" on one end of a strip, 2" from the end. Two inches from the other end of the strip, on the same side, draw one dot. Repeat for numbers 2–10.
2. Cover all strips with clear contact paper or laminate.
3. Cut a 1" slit from the bottom 1" from the end of the strip. Cut a 1" slit from the top 1" from the other end of the strip.
4. Fold the strip so the slits interlock. The strip should resemble a fish.
5. Place a paperclip in the middle of the strip.
6. Tie one end of a length of string to one end of the dowel to represent a fishing rod. Tie the magnet to the other end of the string.

Teaching/ Learning Strategies

Place the fish and fishing rod outdoors or in the dramatic-play area for use during self-directed play periods.

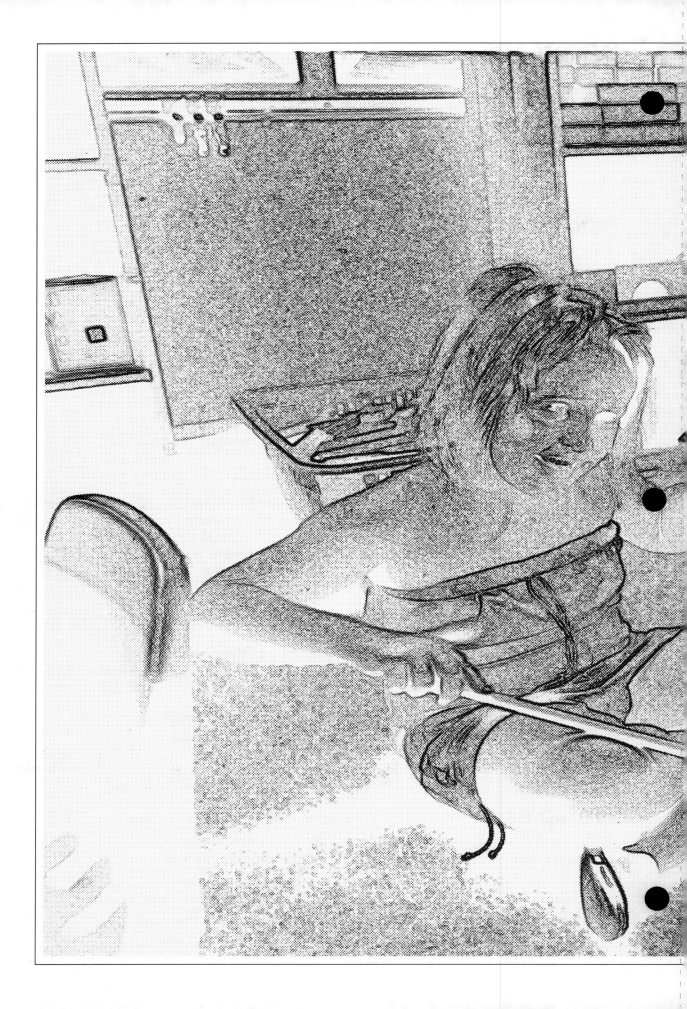

Music

Color-Coded Song Charts

Interest Areas	music language arts
Themes	colors sounds movement feelings music
Teacher Goals	encourage eye-hand coordination promote the development of small motor skills promote visual-discrimination skills encourage music appreciation develop left-to-right progression skills promote rhythm awareness foster color-identification skills
Materials	1 sheet of tagboard colored construction paper colored felt-tip markers glue scissors clear contact paper or laminate

Preparation

1. Choose a simple song that is familiar to the children
2. Print the words of the song on the tagboard, drawing illustrations where necessary (see photograph).
3. Color code the keys on the musical instrument with construction-paper circles. This chart can be used with a piano, xylophone, or organ.
4. Cut out and glue color circles onto the chart to correspond with the appropriate keys on the musical instrument.
5. Cover the chart with clear contact paper or laminate.

Note: After children become familiar with simple color-coded charts, more-complicated songs can be introduced.

Teaching/ Learning Strategies

The chart should be available during self-directed play. If necessary, demonstrate how the colored circles on the chart match the colored circles on the musical instrument. Encourage the children to explore the keyboard. Extend this activity for older children by providing them with colored circles and paper to chart their own original songs.

Color Paddles

Interest Area	music
Themes	sight music shapes colors
Teacher Goals	encourage group cooperation foster music appreciation promote color-identification skills facilitate shape-recognition skills foster listening skills
Materials	sheets of colored construction paper tongue depressors rubber cement clear contact paper or laminate
Preparation	1. Trace and cut as many colored circles as desired, depending on the number of children in the group. 2. Glue two circles of the same color together, placing a tongue depressor between them. 3. Cover the circles with clear contact paper or laminate. 4. Cut around the contact paper or laminate, leaving a 1/4" edge.
Teaching/ Learning Strategies	The color paddles can be used as an aid during music time with songs including color concepts, such as "Mary Wore a Red Dress." The paddles can also be used as a matching or classification activity.

"The Wheels on the Bus" Song Aid

Interest Areas	music language arts
Themes	transportation wheels occupations music
Teacher Goals	promote music appreciation encourage group participation foster listening skills
Materials	yellow and black felt scissors
Preparation	Cut a bus shape and wheels out of felt (see photograph).
Teaching/ Learning Strategies	Use the felt pieces with a flannel board to introduce the song "The Wheels on the Bus" during a group time. Afterwards, place the pieces in the music area for individuals, or small groups of children to use during self-directed play periods.

"The Wheels on the Bus"

1. The wheels on the bus go 'round and 'round, 'round and 'round, 'round and 'round.
    The wheels on the bus go 'round and 'round, all through the town.
2. The door on the bus goes open and shut . . .
3. The driver on the bus says "Move on back" . . .
4. The wipers on the bus go swish, swish, swish . . .

"Five Green-Speckled Frogs" Song Aid

Interest Areas

music
math

● Themes

frogs
animals
water
pond life
rhymes

Teacher Goals

promote music appreciation
facilitate group participation
introduce math concepts through a meaningful experience

Materials

1 sheet of white tagboard
green construction paper
colored felt-tip markers
nylon thread
scissors
tape
clear contact paper or laminate

Preparation

1. Using green construction paper, felt-tip markers, and scissors, draw and cut out five frogs, approximately 5" high.
2. Using the colored felt-tip markers, draw a log and water on the tagboard sheet (see photograph).
3. Cover the sheet of tagboard and the paper frogs with clear contact paper or laminate.
4. Use scissors to poke five evenly spaced holes across the top of the tagboard and five holes 15" directly below the top holes.
5. Thread and tie five lengths of nylon thread through the vertical sets of holes.
6. Tape the backs of the frogs to the nylon thread.

Teaching/ Learning Strategies

Use the props to introduce the poem/song "Five Green-Speckled Frogs." As each verse is sung, pull one string to move a frog into the water. After children are familiar with the rhyme, place the aid in the music area and allow children to use it during self-directed play periods.

Five Green-Speckled Frogs

1. Five green-speckled frogs
   Sat on a speckled log
   Eating the most delicious bugs. Yum! Yum!
   One jumped into the pool
   Where it was nice and cool.
   Then there were four green-speckled frogs.
2. Four green-speckled frogs . . .
3. Three green-speckled frogs . . .
4. Two green-speckled frogs . . .
5. One green-speckled frog . . .

"Little Red Wagon" Song Aid

Interest Area	music

● **Themes**

songs
colors
shapes
transportation
wheels

Teacher Goals

promote color-recognition skills
foster music appreciation
encourage group cooperation
promote dramatic play

Materials

red, blue, yellow, orange, green, purple, black, brown, white, pink, and gray construction paper
scissors
glue
clear contact paper or laminate
1 paintbrush

● **Preparation**

1. Trace and cut a 9" rectangle out of each color of construction paper.
2. Cut and trace one 5" wagon handle.
3. Glue the wagon handle to the red rectangle.
4. Cut and trace two 2 1/2" white circles and two 1" black circles.
5. Glue the black circles to the center of the white circles to represent wheels.
6. Attach the wheels to the red rectangle.
7. Cover all pieces with clear contact paper or laminate.

Teaching/ Learning Strategies

When the song "Little Red Wagon" is sung, let a child volunteer to pretend to paint the wagon. The wagon changes colors as each verse is sung. Allow the children to take turns painting the wagon. After group time, leave the prop out in the classroom. Some children may rediscover it, repeating the activity during a self-directed play period.

"Little Red Wagon"

(sung to the tune of "Skip to my Loo")

Little red wagon painted red
Little red wagon painted red
Little red wagon painted red
What color should it be now?

"Old MacDonald" Song Aid

| **Interest Areas** | music |
| | language arts |

Themes

farms
animals
sounds
music

Teacher Goals

foster music appreciation
promote group participation
promote listening skills

Materials

1 sheet of red tagboard
colored construction paper
colored felt-tip markers
craft knife
scissors
rubber cement or glue
ruler
clear contact paper or laminate

Preparation

1. Trace and cut a barn shape out of the red tagboard sheet (see photograph).
2. Use a craft knife to create six equal-sized doors on the barn.
3. Draw a different farm animal on six squares of construction paper.
4. Glue the animal pictures to the back of the six doors.
5. Use pieces of white construction paper to decorate the main barn door.
6. Cover the barn with clear contact paper or laminate. Use the craft knife to carefully slit open the doors.

Teaching/ Learning Strategies

Use the aid during group time when introducing the song "Old MacDonald." As each verse of the song is sung, open a door to reveal a different animal. After the children are familiar with the song, place the aid in the music area for use during self-directed play periods.

Rhythm Cards for "One, Two, Buckle My Shoe"

| **Interest Areas** | music |
| | math |

Themes

songs
numbers
clothes
rhymes

Teacher Goals

foster music appreciation
promote counting skills
encourage group participation
promote rhythm skills

Materials

15 pieces of tagboard, 9" x 11"
red construction paper
colored felt-tip markers
clear contact paper or laminate

Preparation

1. Cut out fifty-five 1/2" squares out of red construction paper.
2. Glue one red square to a piece of tagboard and print the number "1" and the word "one" on the tagboard. Repeat the process for numbers 2–10.
3. On the five remaining pieces of tagboard, draw a pair of buckle shoes, a door, the action of picking up sticks, the action of laying sticks straight, and a hen.
4. Cover all pieces with clear contact paper or laminate.

Teaching/ Learning Strategies

During group time, introduce the rhythm cards for the chant "One, Two, Buckle My Shoe." Show the cards individually as the related words are spoken. The activity can be extended by having the children use rhythm instruments to accompany the steady beat of the rhyme. Older children can use the instruments to sound out only the numbers in the rhyme.

One, two,
Buckle my shoe;
Three, four,
Shut the door;
Five, six ,
Pick up sticks;
Seven, eight,
Lay them straight;
Nine,ten,
A big fat hen.

Rhythm Sticks

Interest Area

music

Themes

music
sounds
instruments
self-expression

Teacher Goals

encourage music appreciation
introduce new sounds
promote eye-hand coordination
promote the development of small motor skills
provide opportunities to explore rhythms

Materials

For each pair of rhythm sticks:
2 wooden dowels, 1/2" to 1" in diameter, 12" long
acrylic paint
sandpaper

Preparation

1. Sand the dowels, smoothing the ends and sides.
2. Paint the dowels different colors and allow sufficient time for them to dry.

Teaching/ Learning Strategies

Rhythm sticks may be a valuable addition to the classroom. Introduce them during group time and then place them in the music area for use during self-directed play periods. The children can express themselves by tapping out the rhythm of a favorite song. They can also create original songs by exploring and experimenting with the sticks.

Wrist Bells

Interest Area

music

Themes

music
instruments
sounds
communication
bells

Teacher Goals

introduce new sounds
provide opportunities to explore rhythms
foster listening skills
encourage group cooperation

Materials

For each wrist band:
4 jingle bells
1 piece of elastic, 1" wide, 7" long
1 piece of Velcro, 1/2"
thread to match elastic
needle

Preparation

1. Sew four bells on each piece of elastic.
2. Sew the Velcro on each end of the elastic as a fastener.

Teaching/ Learning Strategies

Wrist bells make an interesting addition to the music area. Introduce them during individual or group play. Demonstrate how to fasten the elastic around their wrists. Then create background rhythm, using a record or rhythm instruments. Encourage the children to shake the bells to the rhythm. For variety, have the children attach the bells to their ankles.

July
August
September
October
November
December

Room
Environment

Birthday Balloons

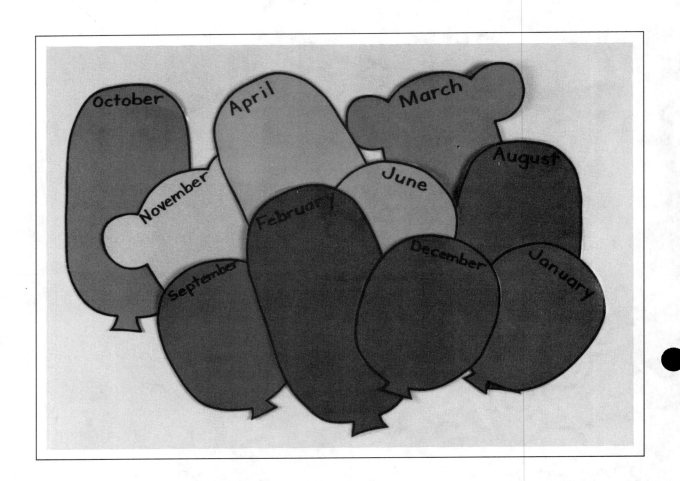

| **Interest Areas** | room environment |
| | language arts |

Themes

birthdays
self-concept
special days
colors

Teacher Goals

provide a print-rich environment
promote self-esteem
reinforce color concepts
introduce the months of the year
promote name-identification skills

Materials

12 sheets of various-colored construction paper
black felt-tip marker
watercolor markers
tape
scissors
clear contact paper or laminate
string

Preparation

1. Using a black felt-tip marker, draw a balloon shape on each sheet of construction paper.
2. Cut out the balloons.
3. Print the name of a different month on each balloon.
4. Cover the balloons with clear contact paper or laminate.
5. Print each child's name and birthday on the appropriate balloon, using a watercolor marker. (The names and birthdates can be wiped off with a damp cloth so that the balloons can be reused each year.)
6. Tape a length of string to each balloon.

Teaching/ Learning Strategies

Hang the birthday balloons on a wall at the children's eye level. At the beginning of each month, point out the names of the children who were born that month.

Birthday Cakes

Interest Areas

room environment
language arts

Themes

birthdays
special days
foods

Teacher Goals

provide a print-rich environment
promote self-esteem
introduce the months of the year
promote name-identification skills

Materials

4 sheets of white tagboard
black felt-tip marker
watercolor markers
scissors
clear contact paper or laminate

Preparation

1. Using a black felt-tip marker, draw twelve 8" x 12" birthday cakes on the white tagboard.
2. Cut out the cakes and decorate them with the markers.
3. Print the name of each month on a cake.
4. Cover the cakes with clear contact paper or laminate.
5. Print each child's name and birthday on the appropriate cake, using a watercolor marker.

Teaching/ Learning Strategies

Decorate the classroom with the birthday cakes, placing them at the children's eye level. As each new month begins, point out each child's name on the birthday cake to promote positive self-esteem.

Birthday Packages

| **Interest Areas** | room environment |
| | language arts |

Themes

birthdays
special days
self-concept

Teacher Goals

introduce the months of the year
promote name-identification skills
provide a print-rich environment
promote self-esteem

Materials

12 sheets of white construction paper, 12" x 18"
black felt-tip marker
watercolor markers
scissors
clear contact paper or laminate

Preparation

1. Using a black felt-tip marker, draw a gift package design on each of the 12 sheets of the paper (see photograph).
2. Cut out the gift packages and decorate with the colored markers.
3. Print the name of each month on a package.
4. Cover the packages with clear contact paper or laminate.
5. Print each child's name and birthday on the appropriate package, using a watercolor marker.

**Teaching/
Learning
Strategies**

Display the packages in the room at the children's eye level. Review the children's birthdays at the beginning of each month.

Birthday Train

Interest Areas

room environment
language arts

Themes

birthdays
self-concept
special days

Teacher Goals

promote self-esteem
provide a print-rich environment
introduce the months of the year
promote name-identification skills

Materials

13 sheets of colored construction paper, 12" x 18"
black felt-tip marker
watercolor markers
clear contact paper or laminate

Preparation

1. Using a black felt-tip marker, draw a train engine and twelve cars on individual sheets of colored construction paper.
2. Cut out the engine and cars and decorate with the colored markers.
3. Print the words "Birthday Train" on the engine.
4. Print the name of each month on a train car.
5. Cover the train pieces with clear contact paper or laminate.
6. Print each child's name and birthday on the appropriate train car, using a watercolor marker.

Teaching/ Learning Strategies

Display the train in the room at the children's eye level. Announce the birthdays at the beginning of each month.

Book-Return Box

Interest Area	room environment
● *Themes*	books libraries
Teacher Goals	encourage the enjoyment of books promote an understanding of how to care for books encourage cooperation
Materials	1 cardboard box, 15" x 10" contact paper black felt-tip permanent marker scissors
Preparation	1. Apply the contact paper to the box. 2. Print "Book Return" on the box, using the felt-tip marker.
● *Teaching/ Learning Strategies*	For programs that include a lending library for parents and children, place the book return in an area that is convenient for both. Otherwise, place the box in the reading area of the classroom.

Interest Areas	room environment signs social studies
Themes	transportation symbols communication
Teacher Goals	foster an understanding of symbols and communication promote the development of language and literacy through a meaningful experience demonstrate how reading and writing are useful communicate to staff and parents the names of children in each car pool encourage verbal expression
Materials	1 sheet of white tagboard black construction paper or stencils and felt-tip markers picture of a car cut from a magazine watercolor markers clear contact paper or laminate glue
Preparation	1. Cut letters from black construction paper for the words "CAR POOL." 2. Glue the letters to the tagboard. 3. Glue the picture of the car to the tagboard. 4. Cover the sign with clear contact paper or laminate. 5. Using watercolor markers, print the names of children who carpool together, along with their driver's name and a telephone number (see photograph).
Teaching/ Learning Strategies	Display the car pool sign at the classroom entrance. This aid is especially helpful for parents and preschool teachers at the beginning of the year.

Interest Areas	room environment social studies
Themes	signs symbols communication
Teacher Goals	promote the development of language and literacy through a meaningful experience encourage letter-recognition skills demonstrate how reading and writing are useful promote self-control
Materials	1 sheet of tagboard white construction paper or stencils and felt-tip markers glue scissors clear contact paper or laminate
Preparation	1. Trace and cut a sign pattern of your choice from the tagboard. 2. Trace and cut letters for the words "Center Closed" or "STOP," from white construction paper and glue them onto the tagboard. Or use stencils and markers to print the words on the sign.
Teaching/ Learning Strategies	Hang the sign in the room at the children's eye level. During group time, explain to the children that the sign has a special meaning. When necessary, provide positive guidance techniques, focusing on the areas that are open for the children to play in.

Daily Schedule Chart

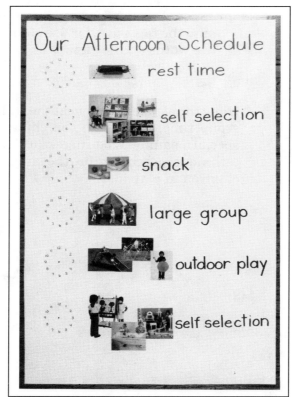

Interest Areas	room environment language arts

Themes	my school letters

Teacher Goals	explain the daily classroom routine promote time concepts create a print-rich environment

Materials	1 or 2 sheets of white or manila tagboard, depending on the classroom schedule colored felt-tip marker pictures of classroom areas and activities cut from educational-supplies catalogs (optional) glue or rubber cement clear contact paper or laminate

Preparation

1. Use the photograph as a guide to make a daily schedule chart. Print a caption for the chart, such as "Daily Schedule" or "Our Morning Schedule," across the top of the tagboard sheet.
2. For each activity time during the day, draw a clock face along the left side of the tagboard sheet. Some teachers may wish to draw the hands of the clocks to depict the time of each activity before the contact paper or laminate is applied. Others may wish to wait until the chart has been laminated and draw in the hands with watercolor markers to allow for time changes.
3. Next to each clock face, glue a picture or make a drawing of the appropriate activity.
4. Print the name of the activity after each picture or drawing.
5. Cover the chart(s) with clear contact paper or laminate.

Teaching/ Learning Strategies

The daily schedule chart is most useful at the beginning of the year to familiarize children with the daily routine. It is also reassuring to new students who arrive after the start of the school year. Introduce the chart at group time and talk about the sequence of activities for the day. Afterwards, display the chart at the children's eye level. Some teachers may want to attach a tagboard arrow to the chart, which can be moved as each new activity begins.

Labels for Classroom Areas or Centers

Interest Areas	room environment
	language arts

Themes

art
music
books
signs

Teacher Goals

encourage letter-recognition skills
provide a print-rich environment
promote word-recognition skills
encourage language development
demonstrate how reading and writing are useful

Materials

1 sheet of tagboard
pictures depicting classroom areas or centers cut from
   educational-supplies catalogs
black felt-tip marker
scissors
glue
clear contact paper or laminate

Preparation

1. Cut out one tagboard piece, approximately 10" x 9", for each classroom area or center—block building, art, storytelling, math, music, science, dramatic play, bathroom, computer, etc.
2. Glue different pictures onto each tagboard piece. For example, the art-center label may contain pictures of markers, scissors, paint, glue, and crayons.
3. Print the name of the area on the bottom of each label.
4. Cover all pieces with clear contact paper or laminate.

Teaching/ Learning Strategies

Place the labels in the appropriate areas of the classroom. Point out the labels to the children and ask them to guess what word(s) they have written on them.

"Number of Children Per Area" Signs

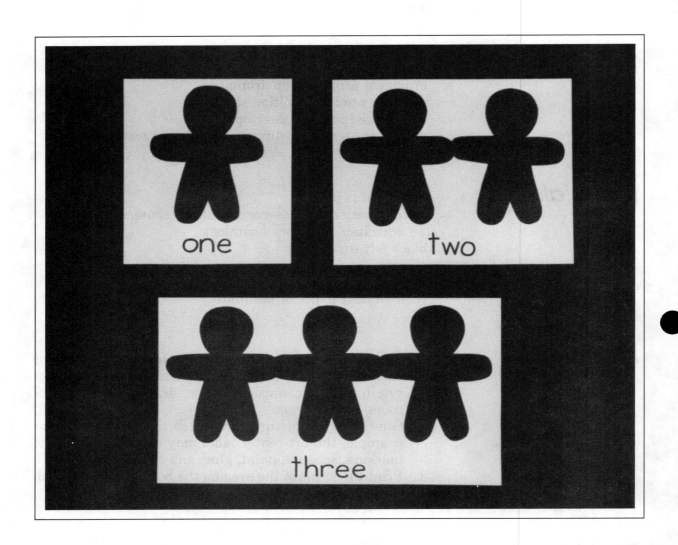

Interest Area   room environment

Themes   counting
numbers

Teacher Goals   foster visual-discrimination skills
encourage one-to-one correspondence
foster self-control by setting clear limits

Materials   pieces of white tagboard, 8" x 10"
black construction paper
rubber cement
black felt-tip marker
scissors
clear contact paper or laminate

Preparation
1. Trace and cut out gingerbread figures from the black construction paper. If necessary, use a cookie cutter or coloring-book to trace a pattern.
2. Print the name of each classroom area or activity on a separate piece of tagboard. Glue the appropriate number of gingerbread figures onto each tagboard piece to represent how many children may participate in each area or activity. Print the word of the number below each set of gingerbread figures (see photograph).
3. Cover all pieces with clear contact paper or laminate.

Teaching/ Learning Strategies
Place the signs in the appropriate classroom areas at the children's eye level.

Number-Line Calendar

Interest Areas

room environment
math

Themes

numbers
patterns
symbols
paper

Teacher Goals

introduce time concepts
promote number-recognition skills
provide a print-rich environment

Materials

1 sheet of colored tagboard
1 piece of white tagboard, 1" x 4"
1 strip of sentence paper, 3" x 74"
black felt-tip marker
glue or rubber cement
scissors
tape
clear contact paper or laminate
1 clothespin

Preparation

1. Cut the colored tagboard horizontally into 4" widths. Tape the 4" widths together so the strips are approximately 75" long (see photograph).
2. Using a black felt-tip marker, print the numbers 1–31 on the strip of sentence paper.
3. Glue the sentence paper strip to the tagboard strip.
4. Cover the entire strip with clear contact paper or laminate.
5. Cut an arrow from the small piece of tagboard. Glue or tape the arrow to a clothespin.

Teaching/ Learning Strategies

Attach the calendar to a wall or bulletin board at the children's eye level. Use the arrow to mark the date. Additional arrows can be constructed to mark holidays, birthdays, and other important dates. In some classrooms, particularly those with older children, the number-line calendar can be used at group time. To foster children's self-esteem, choose a different child each day to move the marker on the calendar.

Interest Area

room environment

Themes

can be adapted to any theme

Teacher Goals

communicate with parents
establish a bond between school and home

Materials

1 sheet of white or manila tagboard
alphabet stencils with uppercase and lowercase letters
1 sheet of colored construction or wrapping paper
1 sheet of white or manila construction paper
scissors
tape
pencil
glue or rubber cement
clear contact paper or laminate
craft knife

Preparation

1. Using the uppercase alphabet stencils, trace and cut out of the colored construction or wrapping paper the letters for the caption "Parent Space."
2. Glue the letters across the top of the tagboard sheet.
3. Fold the single sheet of white construction paper in half and tape two edges to create a pocket.
4. Using the set of lowercase alphabet stencils, trace and cut the letters for the words "Take One."
5. Glue the letters to the construction-paper pocket.
6. Glue the pocket to the lower, right-hand corner of the tagboard sheet.
7. Cover the chart with clear contact paper or laminate.
8. Use the craft knife to carefully slit open the top of the construction-paper pocket.

Teaching/ Learning Strategies

Display the poster near the classroom entrance or lobby of the school. Provide various pamphlets and newsletters on a weekly or monthly basis. Child-development books and parent magazines would also add to the parent space, as would a bulletin board for parents to exchange ideas and recipes and to voice opinions or pose questions.

Lost-and-Found Box

Interest Areas

room environment
social studies

Themes

boxes

Teacher Goals

provide a place for lost items
promote responsibility for belongings

Materials

1 cardboard box, including lid
colored contact paper
1 sheet of construction paper
colored felt-tip markers
scissors
tape

Preparation

1. Cover the box and lid with the colored contact paper.
2. Print the words "Lost and Found" on a rectangular piece of construction paper, using the felt-tip markers.
3. Tape the label to the box lid.

Teaching/ Learning Strategies

The lost-and-found box can be placed near the classroom entrance for parents and children to look through for items that have been misplaced.

Number-and-Set Posters

Interest Areas

room environment
math

Themes

counting
numbers
can be adapted to any theme

Teacher Goals

encourage object-identification skills
promote number-recognition skills

Materials

pieces of tagboard, 14" x 16"
pictures of objects cut from magazines—flowers, snow-
    flakes, raindrops, etc.
scissors
glue or rubber cement
black felt-tip marker
clear contact paper or laminate

Preparation

1. Print a different number on each piece of tagboard, repeating until enough posters have been prepared to suit the children's developmental level.
2. Glue the appropriate number of pictures to the corresponding piece of tagboard.
3. Cover all posters with clear contact paper or laminate.

Teaching/ Learning Strategies

Display posters in the room at the children's eye level. Discuss the numbers and sets during group time.

Clock Decorations

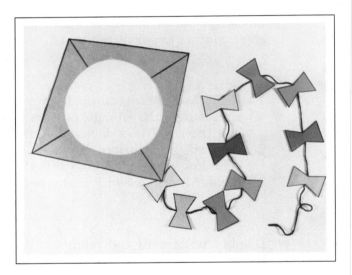

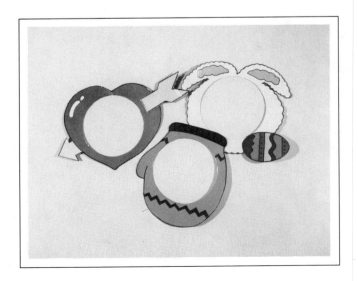

| **Interest Areas** | room environment |
| | language arts |

Themes

seasons
holidays
can be adapted to any theme

Teacher Goals

promote object-identification skills
foster esthetic appreciation
promote color-recognition skills
introduce seasonal symbols

Materials

1 sheet of tagboard
colored felt-tip markers
scissors
ruler or tape measure
pencil
clear contact paper or laminate

Preparation

1. Measure the face of your classroom clock with a ruler or tape measure. Draw a circle of equal diameter on the tagboard, using a pencil.
2. Choose a seasonal symbol from the list below or develop one of your own and sketch it in pencil around the circle (see photograph).
3. Trace over the pencil marks with a felt-tip marker and decorate and color the symbol as desired with additional markers.
4. Cut out the circle, providing a frame for the face of the clock.
5. Cover the tagboard with clear contact paper or laminate.

**Teaching/
Learning
Strategies**

Place the symbol over the face of the clock and call attention to it at group time. If possible, hang the clock at the children's eye level so they can see the numbers on the clock's face.

Symbols for each month might include the following:

January—mitten
February—heart
March—kite or shamrock
April—umbrella or bunny
May—flower
June—sun
July—ice-cream cone
August—watermelon
September—apple
October—pumpkin
November—turkey

Color Crayons

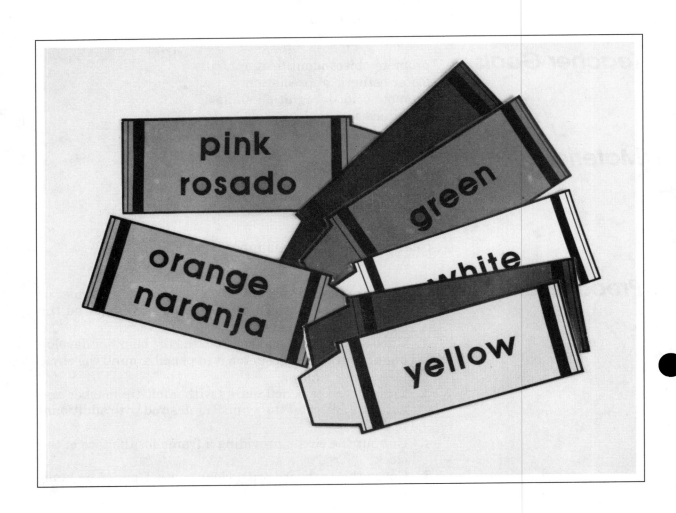

Interest Areas	room environment language arts
Themes	art colors writing tools
Teacher Goals	reinforce color-recognition skills introduce the printed word for each color introduce the Spanish word for each color provide a print-rich environment
Materials	blue, green, yellow, red, white, and pink tagboard black felt-tip marker scissors clear contact paper or laminate
Preparation	1. Measure and cut an 18" x 7" crayon out of each color of tagboard. 2. On one side of each crayon, print the English word for the color. On the other side, print the English and the Spanish word. 3. Cover all pieces with clear contact paper or laminate.
Teaching/ Learning Strategies	During group time, share the crayons with the children by introducing the English and Spanish word for each color. Then place the crayons on the classroom bulletin board or on a wall at the children's eye level.

Science

Absorption Chart

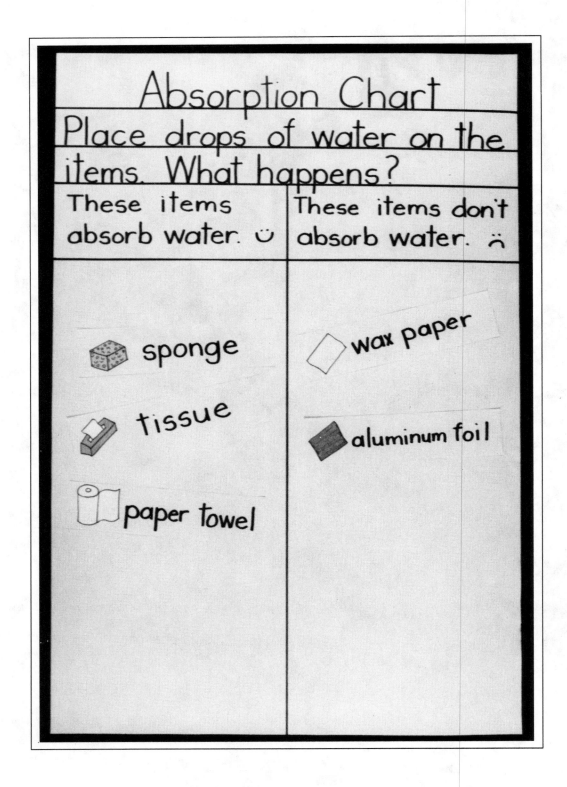

Absorption Chart

Place drops of water on the items. What happens?

These items absorb water. ☺	These items don't absorb water. ☹
sponge	wax paper
tissue	aluminum foil
paper towel	

Interest Areas	science language arts
Themes	water sight
Teacher Goals	introduce a new vocabulary word—"absorption" foster prediction skills introduce science concepts through a meaningful experience provide individual choice
Materials	1 sheet of white or manila tagboard, pieces of tagboard or construction paper, 10" x 2 1/2" colored felt-tip markers ruler clear contact paper or laminate

Preparation

1. Print the words "Absorption Chart" across the top of the tagboard sheet (see photograph).
2. Underneath the title, print the following: "Place drops of water on the items. What happens?"
3. Divide the remaining sheet of tagboard in half with a ruler and marker.
4. On the left-hand side, print the words "These items absorb water."
5. On the right-hand side, print the words "These items don't absorb water."
6. Draw a symbol and print its name on the individual 10" x 2 1/2" pieces of tagboard. Items to be used in the experiment may include a sponge, waxed paper, aluminum foil, a tissue, and paper towel.
7. Cover the chart and the tagboard pieces with clear contact paper or laminate.

Teaching/ Learning Strategies

Gather the materials needed for the activity, including a small container of water and an eyedropper. Display the chart near the activity area. Children put drops of water on each item and determine whether or not the object absorbed the water. They then place the corresponding tagboard piece on the chart. Use tape or adhesive putty to hold the pieces to the chart.

"Things That Move When Blown with a Straw" Chart

Which things will move when you blow them with a straw?	yes ☺	no ☹
tissue		
rock		
block		
tinker toy		
crayon		
paper		
cookie cutter		

Interest Areas	science language arts

Themes	air movement

Teacher Goals	foster prediction skills introduce science concepts through a meaningful experience provide individual choice create a print-rich environment

Materials	1 sheet of manila or white tagboard colored felt-tip markers clear contact paper or laminate

Preparation

1. Use a marker to print the question "Which things will move when you blow them with a straw?" across the top of the tagboard.
2. Draw the symbols and print the names of various objects along the left-hand side of the tagboard (see photograph). Include such items as a tissue, a rock, a block, a tinker toy, a crayon, paper, and a cookie cutter.
3. Draw two vertical columns of squares to the right of the symbols and their names. Above one column of squares print "Yes"; above the other "No."
4. Cover the chart with clear contact paper or laminate.

Teaching/ Learning Strategies

Display the chart near the area where materials have been gathered for the activity. After the children attempt to blow each item with a straw, use a watercolor marker to record the results on the chart.

Sink-or-Float Chart

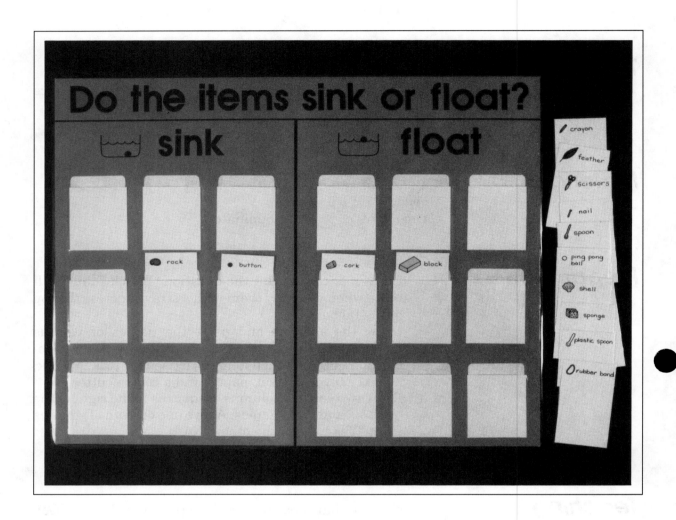

Interest Area	science

Themes

water
sinking/floating

Teacher Goals

introduce the concepts of sinking and floating
expand classification skills
encourage observation and prediction skills
explore the properties of water
introduce science concepts through a meaningful experience
stimulate curiosity

Materials

1 sheet of light-blue tagboard, 10" x 14"
18 library-book pockets
18 white notecards, 3" x 5"
black felt-tip marker
ruler
rubber cement or glue
clear contact paper or laminate

Preparation

1. Print the title "Do the items sink or float?" across the top of the tagboard (see photograph).
2. Underline the title and divide the tagboard in half, using a rule and marker.
3. Print the word "Sink" on the left side and "Float" on the right side of the tagboard.
4. Draw a simple picture symbolizing sinking and floating next to the corresponding word.
5. Glue nine library pockets to the left side and nine to the right side of the tagboard as illustrated in the photograph.
6. On the top of nine notecards, print one name of different objects that sink. On the nine remaining notecards, print one name of different objects that float.
7. Next to each name, draw a simple illustration of the object.
8. Cover all pieces with clear contact paper or laminate.

Teaching/ Learning Strategies

This activity can be placed in the sensory or science area of the classroom. Set up a water table or large dishpan and gather various objects to place in the water—for example, a crayon, rubber band, metal spoon, feather, button, shell, pencil, nail, ping-pong ball, sponge, rock, cork, plastic spoon, scissors, block, clothespin, paintbrush, and marble. Encourage the children to predict which items will sink and which will float. Verify the children's predictions by placing each item in the water and observing what happens. The children then place the corresponding notecard in the appropriate library pocket. Individual children or small groups may enjoy this activity.

Circle-Glider Chart

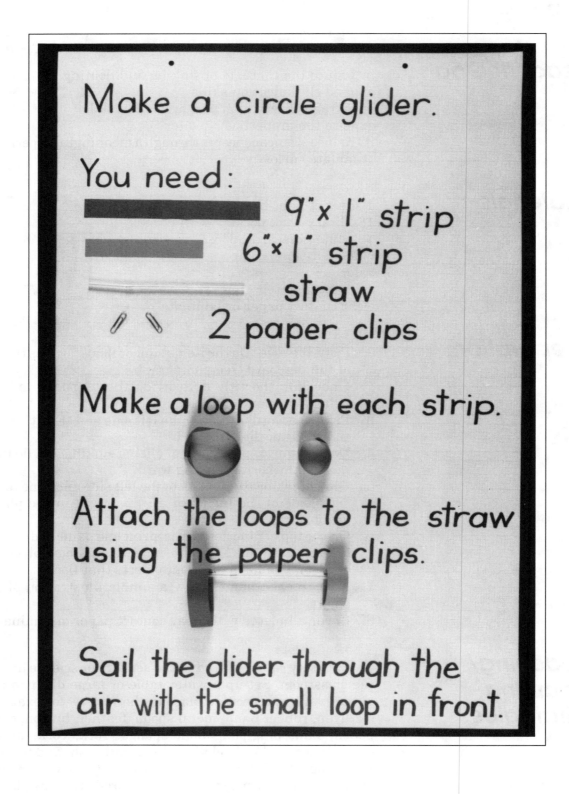

Make a circle glider.

You need:

9" × 1" strip
6" × 1" strip
straw
2 paper clips

Make a loop with each strip.

Attach the loops to the straw using the paper clips.

Sail the glider through the air with the small loop in front.

Interest Areas

science
small motor
language arts

Themes

shapes
movement
air

Teacher Goals

promote the development of small motor skills
provide opportunities for following directions
create a print-rich environment
introduce the movement of an object through air

Materials

1 sheet of manila or white tagboard
1 strip of construction paper, 9" x 1"
1 strip of construction paper, 6" x 1"
1 plastic drinking straw
2 paper clips
glue or rubber cement
black felt-tip marker
clear contact paper or laminate

Preparation

1. Print the directions for making a circle glider on the piece of tagboard (see photograph).

   ### Circle Glider

   a. To make a circle glider you need: 1 strip of construction paper, 9" x 1"
      1 strip of construction paper, 6" x 1"
      1 plastic drinking straw
      2 paper clips
   b. Make a loop with each strip.
   c. Attach the loops to either end of the straw, using the paper clips.
   d. Sail the glider through the air with the small loop in front.
2. Glue the paper strips, straw, and paper clips to the chart.
3. Cover the chart with clear contact paper or laminate.

Teaching/ Learning Strategies

Display the chart above a table with the necessary materials. After the children make the circle gliders, they can be used outdoors or in a large indoor area.

Height-and-Weight Chart

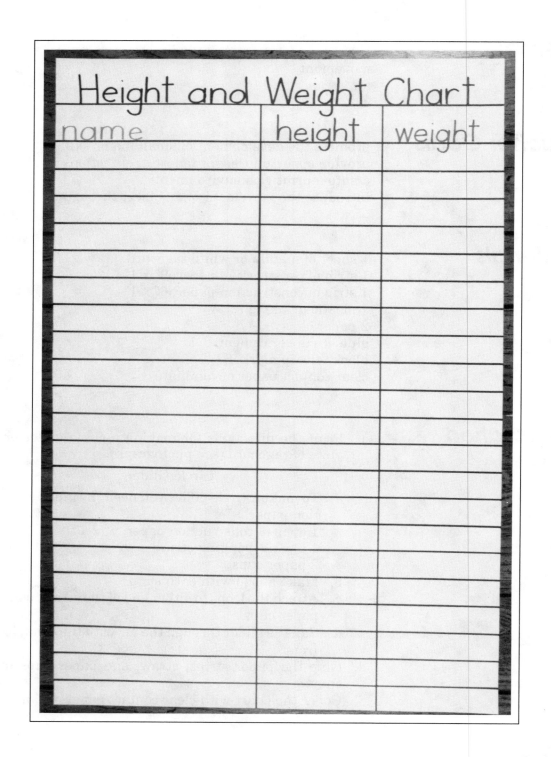

Interest Areas	science language arts

Themes	my body self-concept numbers

Teacher Goals	foster self-esteem promote concepts of height and weight provide a print-rich environment

Materials	1 sheet of white or manila tagboard ruler colored felt-tip markers clear contact paper or laminate.

Preparation

1. Print the caption "Height and Weight Chart" across the top of the tagboard sheets.
2. Use the ruler and a felt-tip marker to make three vertical columns.
3. Label the first column "Name," the second column "Height," and third column "Weight" (see photograph).
4. Use a ruler and marker to make horizontal lines on which each child's name, height, and weight will eventually be recorded.
5. Cover the chart with clear contact paper or laminate.

Teaching/ Learning Strategies

Display the chart in the science area near a scale and tape measure. Use a watercolor marker to record each child's name, height, and weight.

Worm-Farm Chart

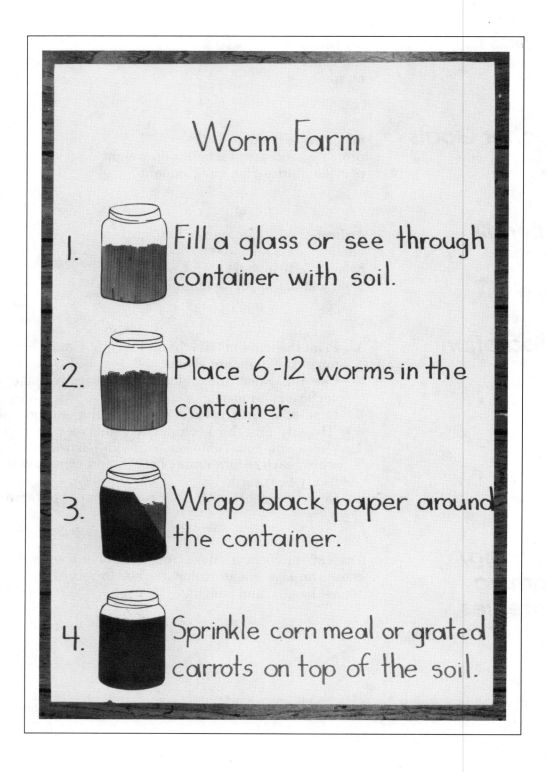

Worm Farm

1. Fill a glass or see through container with soil.

2. Place 6-12 worms in the container.

3. Wrap black paper around the container.

4. Sprinkle corn meal or grated carrots on top of the soil.

Interest Areas

science
language arts

Themes

soil
gardens
plants
animals

Teacher Goals

foster an appreciation for nature
increase observation skills
introduce science concepts through a meaningful experience
demonstrate how reading and writing are useful
create a print-rich environment

Materials

1 sheet of manila or white tagboard
colored felt-tip markers
clear contact paper or laminate

Preparation

1. On the sheet of tagboard, use the markers to print the directions and draw the corresponding illustrations (see photograph).

WORM FARM

a. Fill a glass or clear container with soil.
b. Place 6—12 worms in the container.
c. Sprinkle cornmeal or grated carrot on top of the soil.
d. Wrap black paper around the container.

2. Cover the chart with clear contact paper or laminate.

Teaching/ Learning Strategies

Gather the materials needed and allow children to assist in preparing a worm farm. Inform the children that the black paper wrapped around the jar helps to keep the light out of the jar, encouraging the worms to locate near the outside of the container. Periodically remove the black paper for a brief time to observe the worms and their trails. After the children have lost interest in the farm, free the worms outdoors in a garden or flower bed. Display the worm-farm chart at the children's eye level in the science area.

Carrot-Cake Recipe Chart

Carrot Cake

Mix these ingredients in a bowl.

add 1 at a time

Measure these ingredients and put them in a different bowl.

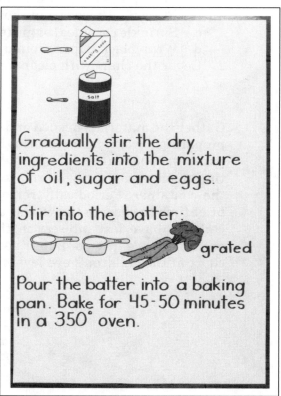

Gradually stir the dry ingredients into the mixture of oil, sugar and eggs.

Stir into the batter:

grated

Pour the batter into a baking pan. Bake for 45-50 minutes in a 350° oven.

Interest Areas	science
	math
	language arts

Themes

cooking
food
vegetables
gardens
Easter
occupations
recipes

Teacher Goals

increase self-esteem
provide opportunities for following directions
increase letter/word-recognition skills
promote group cooperation
foster eye-hand coordination
promote left-right progression skills
encourage observation skills
introduce science concepts through a meaningful experience

Materials

1 sheet of tagboard
colored felt-tip markers
clear contact paper or laminate

Preparation

1. Use the felt-tip markers to print the recipe and draw the corresponding illustrations on the tagboard (see photograph).

Carrot Cake

1 1/2 cups oil
2 cups sugar
4 eggs
2 cups flour
1 teaspoon baking powder
1 teaspoon baking soda
1/2 teaspoon salt
2 cups grated carrots

Combine all the ingredients and pour the batter into a 9" x 13" pan. Bake for 45—50 minutes in a 350° pre-heated oven.

2. Cover the chart with clear contact paper or laminate.

Teaching/ Learning Strategies

Collect all of the ingredients and utensils. Display the recipe chart at the children's eye level and follow the steps as written. Allow the children to participate. While preparing the batter, keep referring to the chart as you progress from step to step.

Orange-Shake Recipe Chart

Interest Areas

science
math
language arts

Themes

food
fruits and vegetables

Teacher Goals

provide opportunities to decode symbols and written words
introduce math and science concepts through a meaningful
    experience
encourage conversation while at play
foster social skills
promote the development of language and literacy through
    a meaningful experience.

Materials

1 sheet of tagboard
colored felt-tip markers
clear contact paper or laminate

Preparation

1. Print the words "Orange Shake" across the top of the
    tagboard.
2. Print the recipe on the chart, leaving space to draw
    pictures of the ingredients.

Orange Shake

6 ounces frozen orange juice
1 cup cold water
1 cup milk
2 teaspoons sugar
1 teaspoon vanilla
5—10 ice cubes

Blend the ingredients until the ice is crushed and the
mixture is thick.

3. Cover the chart with clear contact paper or laminate.

Teaching/ Learning Strategies

Place the recipe chart, ingredients, and utensils to prepare
the orange shake in the cooking area. Begin by telling the
children what you will be making. Prepare the orange
shake during the self-directed period with a small group of
children. As each ingredient is added, refer to the chart,
following the directions as outlined.

Hand Rests

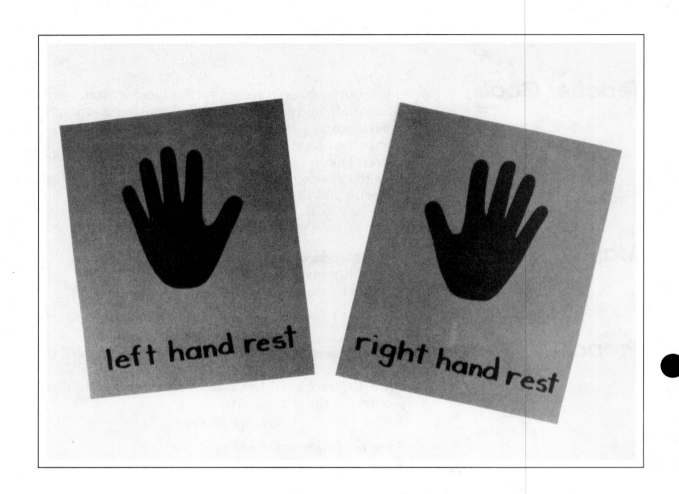

Interest Area

science

Themes

hot and cold
cooking
food

Teacher Goals

increase safety awareness during cooking activities
foster classroom safety
stimulate language skills
promote self-control and cooperation

Materials

black construction paper
black felt-tip marker
2 pieces of red tagboard, 8" x 10 1/2"
rubber cement
clear contact paper or laminate

Preparation

1. Cut a right hand and a left hand, child sized, out of black construction paper.
2. Glue the left hand to the middle of one sheet of red tagboard.
3. Directly under the hand, print the words "Left Hand Rest."
4. Glue the right hand to the middle of the other piece of red tagboard.
5. Below the hand, print the words "Right Hand Rest."
6. Cover both pieces with clear contact paper or laminate.

Teaching/ Learning Strategies

Hand rests can be used during cooking activities to teach the concepts of hot and cold and to reinforce safe classroom practices. Demonstrate to the children how to place one hand on the rest while using the other hand to stir, turn, or mix, over a heat source. Explain to the children how the hand rests prompt safety. After the cooking activity, place the hand rests in the dramatic-play area for use during self-directed play.

Interest Area

science

Themes

pond life
animals

Teacher Goals

introduce the life cycle of a frog
promote the development of small motor skills
foster visual-discrimination skills
foster an appreciation of nature
introduce science concepts through a meaningful experience

Materials

1 sheet each of white and green tagboard
colored felt-tip markers
1 brass fastener
glue or rubber cement
craft knife
clear contact paper or laminate

Preparation

1. Print the words "Frog Life Cycle" across the top of the white tagboard sheet.
2. Draw the six stages of frog development in a circle on the white tagboard (see photograph).
3. Cut the sheet of green tagboard into a circle, approximately 21" in diameter.
4. Cut a 6" section out of the green circle.
5. Cover both tagboard pieces separately with clear contact paper or laminate.
6. Trim the contact paper or laminate from the green circle, using a craft knife.
7. Using a brass fastener in the center, attach the green circle to the middle of the frog-development circle on the white tagboard.

Teaching/ Learning Strategies

Rotate the green wheel on the chart, revealing one stage of the frog life cycle at a time. Draw the children's attention to the difference between each stage. Extend this activity by placing frogs or tadpoles in the science area, providing an opportunity for the children to observe and care for them.

Hatching-Eggs Countdown

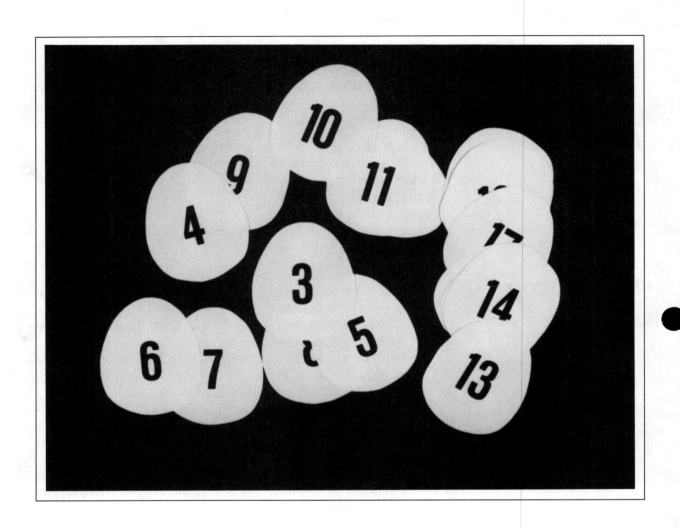

| **Interest Areas** | science |
| | math |

Themes

farm animals
chickens
birds
Easter
spring

Teacher Goals

increase number-recognition skills
introduce the development of hatching eggs
foster visual-discrimination skills
provide opportunities to track the passage of time

Materials

white construction paper
black felt-tip marker
scissors
clear contact paper or laminate

Preparation

1. Trace and cut out twenty-one 5" x 6" eggs from the white construction paper.
2. Write a number on each egg from 1—21, representing the incubation period for chick eggs.
3. Cover all pieces with clear contact paper or laminate.

Teaching/ Learning Strategies

Display the eggs sequentially in the science area near the incubator. Each day at group time, remove the last egg. For example, on the first day, remove the egg with the number 21; on the second day, the egg with the number 20. Continue the countdown until the chicks hatch.

Insect Net

Interest Area	science
Themes	insects and spiders nature
Teacher Goals	introduce science concepts through a meaningful experience promote an appreciation of nature encourage observation skills stimulate curiosity
Materials	2 cardboard circles, 12" in diameter 1 yard of sheer netting material scissors string

Preparation

1. Designate one of the circles as the top of the net. Pierce a hold in the center and thread a long string through the hole—long enough to suspend the net from the ceiling. Tie a knot at the bottom of the string.
2. Place the netting on the floor and position the top and bottom circles 2 1/2' apart. Wrap the netting around the circles, allowing it to overlap several inches (see photograph).
3. Wrap a piece of string around the fabric underneath the bottom circle and tie a knot.
4. Wrap another piece of string around the fabric above the top circle and tie a knot.

Teaching/ Learning Strategies

Suspend the insect net from the ceiling near or in the science area. As children find butterflies or moths, the insects can be placed in the net for observation. To do this, slide your hand through the overlapped fabric and insert the insect. If possible, place a small branch in the bottom of the net for the insects. Release the insects to the outdoors after two days of observation. Extend the activity by placing a cocoon or chrysalis in the net. Provide informational books on insects to share with the children.

Terrarium

Interest Areas

science
room environment

Themes

plants
gardening
how things grow

Teacher Goals

encourage observation skills
foster an appreciation of nature
introduce the care of plants
promote cooperation skills in caring for the plant

Materials

1 plastic 2-liter bottle
potting soil
scissors
plant

Preparation

1. After soaking in warm water, remove the black base from a plastic 2-liter bottle, using sharp scissors.
2. Cut off the top third of the bottle.
3. Place the soil and the plant into the bottle base.
4. Insert the plastic bottle into the base upside down, thereby creating a dome to cover the plant.

Teaching/ Learning Strategies

Place the plant in the science area or use it to decorate the room. One child can be responsible for watering the plant as needed. If desired, prepare a chart and place it by the plant, recording how often the plant is watered.

Leaf Book

Interest Areas

science
language arts

Themes

trees
plants
books
leaves
nature

Teacher Goals

promote observation skills
foster an appreciation of nature
increase awareness of plant growth

Materials

various dried leaves
1 sheet of white tagboard
scissors
black felt-tip marker
ruler
clear contact paper or laminate
paper punch
two loose-leaf rings

Preparation

1. Cut the tagboard into 10" x 12" pieces.
2. Using half of the tagboard pieces, create frames by removing the centers leaving 1 1/4" around the edges (see photograph).
3. Center a leaf within each frame and cover with contact paper or laminate on both sides of the frame.
4. If desired, print the name of each leaf on the lower edge of the frame.
5. Arrange the pages of the leaf book, starting with a solid piece of tagboard for the cover and placing a solid piece of tagboard in between the leaf-framed pages.
6. Punch two holes along the left edge of the tagboard pages.
7. Bind the book together using two loose-leaf rings.
8. Print the words "Leaf Book" on the cover.

Teaching/ Learning Strategies

Place the leaf book in the science or language-arts area. Encourage the children to look, feel, and compare the individual leaves. Use magnifying glasses to add interest to the activity.

Felt Weather Recorder

| **Interest Areas** | science |
| | language arts |

Themes

weather
symbols
seasons

Teacher Goals

stimulate language skills
reinforce the concept of weather
introduce the effects of different weather conditions
encourage an interest in weather conditions

Materials

1 piece of blue felt, 53" x 15"
gray, white, and yellow felt scraps
aluminum foil
scissors
craft glue
fabric spray

Preparation

1. Cut the letters for the words "Monday", "Tuesday", "Wednesday", "Thursday", and "Friday" from black felt.
2. Attach the days of the week in the proper sequence across the top of the blue piece of felt (see photograph).
3. Cut white clouds, gray clouds, yellow suns, and white snowflakes from felt.
4. Cut raindrops from aluminum foil and mount them on felt scraps.
5. Spray all the pieces with a fabric spray to prevent soiling.

Teaching/ Learning Strategies

Place the weather recorder in the group-time area. Ask a different child each day to place the appropriate weather symbols on the chart. At the end of the week, encourage the children to count how many days were sunny, cloudy, etc.

Temperature Graph

Temperature Graph

Day / Fahrenheit Temperature	Monday	Tuesday	Wednesday	Thursday	Friday
100°					
90°					
80°					
70°					
60°					
50°					
40°					
30°					
20°					
10°					
0°					
-10°					
-20°					
-30°					

Interest Area	science

● Themes

seasons
weather
hot/cold
numbers

Teacher Goals

reinforce the concept of weather
introduce the relationship of temperature to weather
introduce graphing skills

Materials

1 piece of tagboard, 18" x 24"
black felt-tip marker
rules
clear contact paper or laminate

Preparation

1. Print the title "Temperature Graph" across the top of the tagboard (see photograph).
2. Below the title, print the days of the week.
3. Along the left-hand side, print the numbers representing temperatures 100° to -30°.
4. Using a ruler, draw vertical lines to section off the days of the week; draw horizontal lines for each degree.
5. Cover the tagboard with clear contact paper or laminate.

Teaching/ Learning Strategies

Children need to be provided with many classroom opportunities to see how writing is useful. Graphing the temperature each day during group time is one way to do this. This graph would probably be more appropriate during opening time with kindergarten-age children.

Thermometer

Interest Area	science

● Themes

weather
seasons
hot/cold
numbers

Teacher Goals

reinforce weather concepts
encourage an interest in science
introduce new vocabulary words—"fahrenheit" and "centigrade"

Materials

1 sheet of white tagboard
white elastic, 1/2" x 21"
red ribbon, 1/2" x 21"
black felt-tip marker
pictures of children in different seasonal clothing cut from
magazines
1 red circle, 3" in diameter
thread
needle
glue
craft knife
clear contact paper or laminate

Preparation

1. Draw the outline of a thermostat on the tagboard.
2. Use the black felt-tip marker to record fahrenheit and centigrade temperatures on the tagboard (see photograph).
3. Attach pictures of children in seasonal clothing that correspond with approximate temperatures.
4. Use a craft knife to cut a 1" slit at the top and the bottom of the thermometer.
5. Glue the red circle to the bottom of the thermometer.
6. Cover the tagboard with clear contact paper or laminate.
7. Sew one end of the red ribbon to one end of the white elastic.
8. Thread the ribbon/elastic through the tagboard slits and sew ends together to form a loop.

● Teaching/ Learning Strategies

Place the thermometer in the group-time area. Discuss the weather on a daily basis, moving the elastic to correspond to the outdoor temperature.

Magic Mirror Pictures

Interest Area	science
● *Themes*	I'm special pictures
Teacher Goals	encourage exploration skills promote the understanding that a mirror creates a reflection foster prediction skills
Materials	colored tagboard squares, 6" x 6" white construction-paper squares, 5" x 5" colored felt-tip markers small hand mirror scissors rubber cement
Preparation	1. Draw half of an object on a 5" x 5" piece of white construction paper—for example, a face, star, fish, rainbow, dress, butterfly, ice cream cone, or heart (see photograph). 2. Mount the 5" x 5" square on a 6" x 6" piece of colored tagboard, using rubber cement.
Teaching/ Learning Strategies	Discovery or science activities should be available on a daily basis for use during self-directed play periods. To use the magic mirror pictures, the children place the mirror on the edge of the picture. The reflection of the picture will appear in the mirror and, thus, make the picture look whole.

Reflection Cards

Interest Area

science

Themes

sight
experiments
light
communication

Teacher Goals

foster eye-hand coordination
promote experimentation with light and reflection
encourage observation skills
introduce a new vocabulary word—"reflection"

Materials

aluminum foil
black construction paper
scissors
glue

Preparation

1. Cut 8" x 10" cards out of the construction paper.
2. Cut aluminum foil into different shapes and sizes.
3. Glue a variety of shapes onto the cards. When gluing, be careful to expose the shiny side of the foil.

Teaching/ Learning Strategies

Reflection cards make an interesting addition to the science table. When held at an angle next to a wall or table, light is reflected from the foil to the surface.

Colored Glasses

Interest Area

science

Themes

colors
our senses

Teacher Goals

promote color-identification skills
promote visual-discrimination skills
encourage active exploration of materials
encourage experimentation with cause-and-effect relation-
    ships

Materials

tagboard
rubber cement
sheets of colored acetate or cellophane

Preparation

1. Trace a pattern for glasses and cut out of the tagboard
   (see photograph).
2. Cut two circles, 2" in diameter, representing lenses out
   of the acetate or cellophane.
3. Glue the lenses to the back of the glass frame.

Teaching/ Learning Strategies

Place the colored glasses on the science table. For variation,
put them by the easel to be worn while painting.

Pail-and-Shovel
Color Match

Interest Areas

science
math
small motor

Themes

colors
summer fun
beaches
sand and soil

Teacher Goals

foster color-recognition skills
promote eye-hand coordination
promote the development of small motor skills
encourage one-to-one correspondence

Materials

pink, white, light-green, dark-green, brown, red, yellow, orange, dark-blue, and light-blue tagboard
black felt-tip marker
craft knife
scissors
clear contact paper or laminate

Preparation

1. Trace and cut out of each sheet of tagboard a 6" x 8" pail and a 2 1/2" x 6" shovel (see photograph). The number prepared will depend on the developmental level of the children.
2. Cut out a 5" circle at the top of every pail.
3. Cover all pieces with clear contact paper or laminate.
4. Using the craft knife, cut away the contact paper or laminate from the circle at the top of each pail.

Teaching/ Learning Strategies

This is an interesting activity for self-directed play periods. Place the materials on a table in the science, math, or small-motor area. If needed, show the children how to match the pail and shovel. Ask questions such as "What pail matches this shovel?" This is a good activity for reviewing color skills.

Paintbrush-and-Bucket
Color Match

Interest Areas

science
math

Themes

colors
occupations
community helpers
brushes

Teacher Goals

promote color-recognition skills
foster eye-hand coordination
promote small motor skills
improve color-differentiation skills
encourage one-to-one correspondence

Materials

4 sheets of white tagboard
colored felt-tip markers
craft knife
scissors
clear contact paper or laminate

Preparation

1. Trace and cut five 1/2" x 6 1/2" paint cans and five 3" x 6" paintbrushes out of the tagboard (see photograph). The number prepared will depend on the developmental level of the children.
2. Cut out a 4" oval from the top of each paint can.
3. Decorate the paint cans and paintbrushes with colored markers, making sure there is a colored paintbrush that corresponds with each colored paint can.
4. Cover all pieces with clear contact paper or laminate.
5. Using the craft knife, cut away the contact paper or laminate from the oval at the top of each paint can.

Teaching/ Learning Strategies

This activity can be placed in the science, math or small-motor area for use during self-directed play periods. Observe the children and provide assistance if needed. An individual child or a group of children may participate. These teaching materials can also be used to develop an effective child-involvement bulletin board. The bulletin caption should read "Matching." Attach the buckets to the bulletin board. Place the brushes in a small basket under the bulletin board. The children can insert the brushes into the matching paint cans.

Marble Track Game

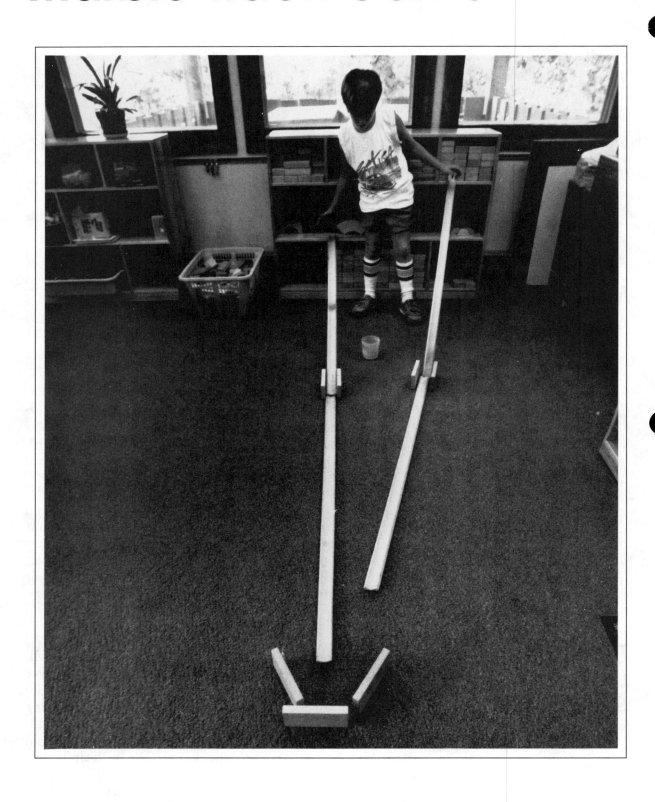

Interest Area	science

Themes

games
balls

Teacher Goals

promote group cooperation
promote the development of small motor skills
foster eye-hand coordination
introduce the concepts of gravity/force
provide opportunities for taking turns
promote problem-solving skills

Materials

several lengths of cove molding (available at building-supply stores)
marbles or ping-pong balls
sandpaper
paint or varnish (optional)

Preparation

1. Sand the moldings to make them smooth.
2. Paint or varnish if desired.

Teaching/ Learning Strategies

Prop the moldings from tables or cabinets at an angle. The children can place marbles or ping-pong balls on the moldings and visually track the movement.

Wave Jar

Interest Area	science

Themes

water
ocean
movement

Teacher Goals

encourage observation skills
promote eye-hand coordination
create an understanding of movement
introduce science concepts through a meaningful experience

Materials

1 clear plastic container
mineral oil
blue food coloring
water
rubber cement

Preparation

1. Fill the plastic container halfway with water and add several drops of blue food coloring.
2. Fill the remainder of the container with mineral oil.
3. Pour rubber cement into the cap of the container.
4. Screw on the cap, wiping off the excess rubber cement. Allow it to dry before the children use it.

Teaching/ Learning Strategies

The wave jar can be prepared and placed in the science area of the classroom. The children will learn about their physical world as they playfully interact with the jar. Waves can be created by slowly tilting the container back and forth. If needed, the teacher may serve as a guide or facilitator, demonstrating an interest in the jar and showing the children how to create waves.

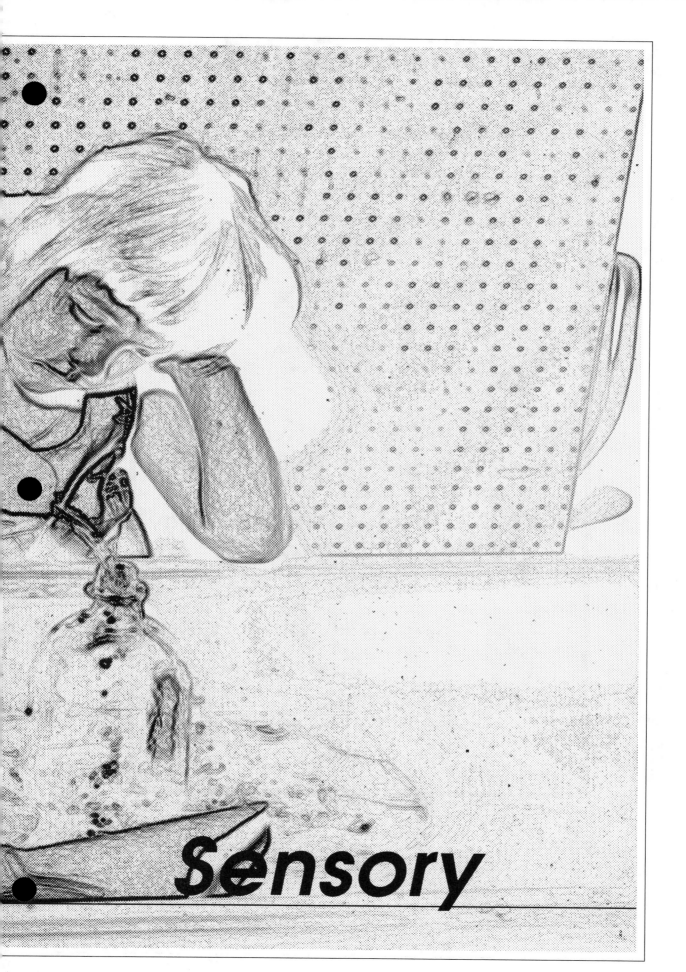

Sensory

Bubble-Prints Chart

Bubble Prints

In a cup mix these ingredients.

Place a straw in the cup.

Blow bubbles until they begin to overflow.

Remove straw and place paper over the bubbles.

Remove the paper from the bubbles.

Interest Areas

sensory
art
science
language arts
math

Themes

water
bubbles
air
colors
sight

Teacher Goals

stimulate the senses
foster art appreciation
promote color-identification skills
provide individual choice
create a print-rich environment

Materials

1 sheet of manila or white tagboard
colored felt-tip markers
clear contact paper or laminate

Preparation

1. On the sheet of tagboard, use the markers to print the directions and draw the corresponding illustrations (see photograph).

Bubble Prints

   a. In a cup, mix the following ingredients:
      1/2 cup water
      2 tablespoons liquid dish soap
      1 tablespoon food coloring
   b. Place a straw in the cup.
   c. Blow bubbles until they begin to overflow.
   d. Remove the straw and place paper over the bubbles.
   e. Remove the paper from the bubbles.
2. Cover the chart with clear contact paper or laminate.

Teaching/ Learning Strategies

Gather the materials needed to make bubble prints. Provide smocks and protective coverings for tables and place the bubbles in the sensory, art, or science area. Display the chart at the children's eye level. Before the activity, encourage the children to practice the process of blowing air through a straw.

Bubble Recipe Chart

Interest Areas

sensory
science

Themes

water
air
bubbles

Teacher Goals

stimulate the senses
promote observation skills
provide opportunities for following directions
provide a print-rich environment

Materials

1 sheet of manila or white tagboard
colored felt-tip markers
clear contact paper or laminate

Preparation

1. On the sheet of tagboard, use the markers to print the directions and draw the corresponding illustrations (see photograph).

Bubble Recipe

a. In a bucket, mix the following ingredients:
   8 cups water
   3/4 cup liquid dish soap
   1/4 cup glycerine
b. Use the solution to make bubbles
2. Cover the chart with clear contact paper or laminate.

Teaching/ Learning Strategies

Following the directions on the chart, prepare the bubble solution with assistance from the children. Provide various bubble makers with the solution, such as plastic six-pack soda rings, pipe cleaners, plastic berry baskets, and commercial bubble rings.

Goop Recipe Chart

Recipe for "Goop"

Pour two inches of cornstarch into a container.

Add 4 drops of food coloring.

Slowly add and stir enough water to make a thick mixture.

Enjoy playing with the "goop" using your fingers, spoons, bowls, and strainers.

Interest Areas

sensory
science
language arts

Themes

touch
colors

Teacher Goals

promote tactile awareness
foster an awareness of changes in a substance
provide individual choices

Materials

1 sheet of white or manila tagboard
colored felt-tip markers
clear contact paper or laminate

Preparation

1. On the sheet of tagboard, use the markers to print the directions and draw the corresponding illustrations (see photograph).

Goop Recipe

   a. Pour 2" of cornstarch into a container.
   b. Add four drops of food coloring.
   c. Slowly add and stir enough water to make a thick mixture.
   d. Enjoy playing with the goop, using your fingers, spoons, bowls, and strainers.
2. Cover the chart with clear contact paper or laminate.

Teaching/ Learning Strategies

Gather the materials needed and display the chart at the children's eye level. Allow the children to assist you in preparing the goop. Refer to the chart, following the directions as outlined.

Fingerpainting in a Bag

Interest Areas	sensory
	art
	science
	small motor

Themes	art
	colors
	painting

Teacher Goals	encourage creative expression
	promote color-identification skills
	encourage mixing colors
	promote the development of small motor skills

Materials	gallon-size, self-sealing plastic bags
	masking tape
	tempera or finger paint

Preparation

1. Place 1/4 cup of fingerpaint in each bag.
2. Seal the bag, adding masking tape around the edge for extra protection.

Teaching/ Learning Strategies

Place the bags of fingerpaint on a table in the art, small-motor, or science area. If needed, show the children how to use the bag. This activity can be extended by placing two colors of tempera paint in a bag and encouraging the children to mix them.

Individual Feely Boxes

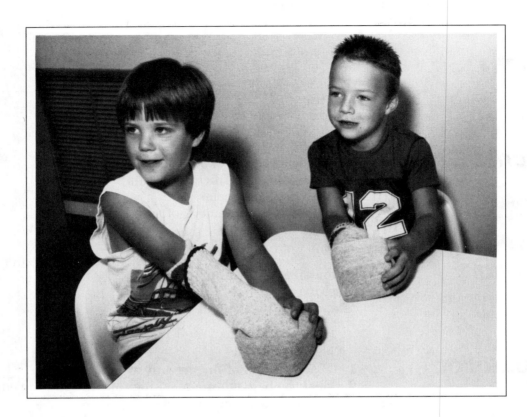

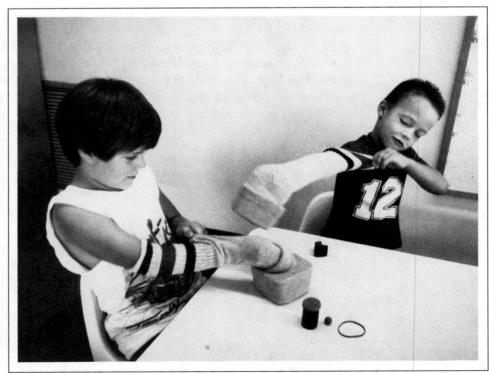

Interest Areas

sensory
science
language arts

Theme

touch

Teacher Goals

promote tactile awareness
promote the development of small motor skills
stimulate curiosity
foster prediction skills

Materials

For each feely box:
1 adult-size tube sock
1 pint-size plastic container (such as freezer food containers
   or empty yogurt or cottage cheese containers)

Preparation

Insert the plastic container all the way to the bottom of the
sock.

Teaching/ Learning Strategies

Gather several small items to place in the feely boxes—for
example, a cotton ball, clothespin, crayon, rock, small block,
coin, toy car, etc. Place the filled feely boxes in the science
area. To use, the children insert their hands into the socks
and attempt to identify the objects by touch. The items can
then be pulled out of the feely boxes to verify their guesses.

Scoops

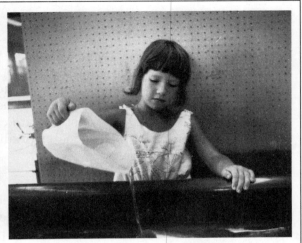

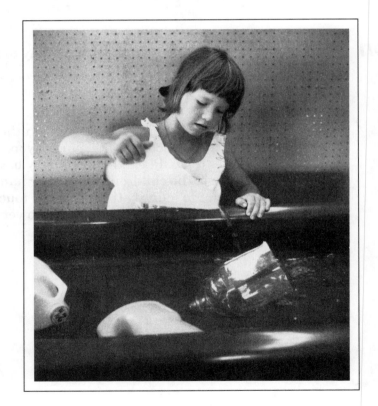

Interest Areas

sensory
science

Themes

tools
shovels and scoops
sand and soil
water

Teacher Goals

promote the development of small motor skills
promote eye-hand coordination
encourage tactile awareness
encourage experimentation
introduce the use of recyclable materials

Materials

empty plastic containers (such as soda, shampoo, dish-
    washing detergent, bleach bottles, etc.)
scissors or craft knife
sandpaper

Preparation

1. Wash the containers.
2. Using scissors or a craft knife, cut the bottoms off the
   plastic containers at different angles (see photograph).
3. If necessary, use sandpaper to smooth the edges of the
   plastic.

Teaching/ Learning Strategies

Children need sensory opportunities on a daily basis. Place
scoops on the sensory table or in the sandbox to encourage
active exploration. These tools can be used to manipulate
sand, dirt, water, flour, beans, etc.

Sifters

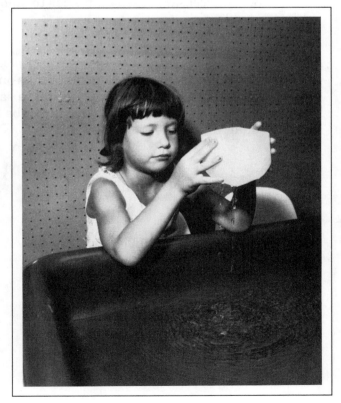

Interest Areas	sensory
	science
	small motor

Themes	cooking
	sand and soil
	water

Teacher Goals

encourage tactile sense awareness
promote experimentation
encourage prediction skills
promote the development of small motor skills

Materials

various plastic bottles, such as milk, dish soap, detergent, shampoo, etc.
scissors or craft knife
different sizes of nails or map tacks

Preparation

1. Wash the plastic bottles.
2. Using scissors or a craft knife, cut 2" to 3" off from the bottom of the container. The top portion can be used as a scoop or funnel.
3. Push a nail or a mop tack several times through the bottom of the container. For variety, make sifters of varying hole sizes.

Teaching/ Learning Strategies

Use the sifters in the sensory area or at the water table with a variety of materials, such as water, sand, soil, or gravel. The children should be encouraged to explore the properties of the materials with the sifters. If sifters of varying hole sizes are provided, encourage the children to observe the size of the hole in relation to how slowly or quickly the material sifts.

Small Motor

Egg-Shaped Wallpaper Puzzles

Interest Areas

small motor
science

Themes

Easter
shapes
paper
designs

Teacher Goals

promote visual-discrimination skills
foster eye-hand coordination
promote the development of small motor skills
encourage independent play

Materials

wallpaper scraps
scissors
clear contact paper or laminate

Preparation

1. Cut oval shapes out of wallpaper scraps.
2. Using a variety of creative patterns—zigzag, wavy, straight edge—cut the ovals in half. The complexity of the cutting patterns should suit the developmental needs of the children.
3. Cover with clear contact paper or laminate.

Teaching/ Learning Strategies

This activity can be done individually or in small groups of children. The children select oval pieces, matching them with their corresponding halves. Provide the children with uninterrupted time to persist at the activity. For children who are unable to fit the puzzle pieces together, the adult needs to act as a facilitator, providing clues and suggestions. Once mastered, the children may initiate and repeat the process.

Valentine Puzzles

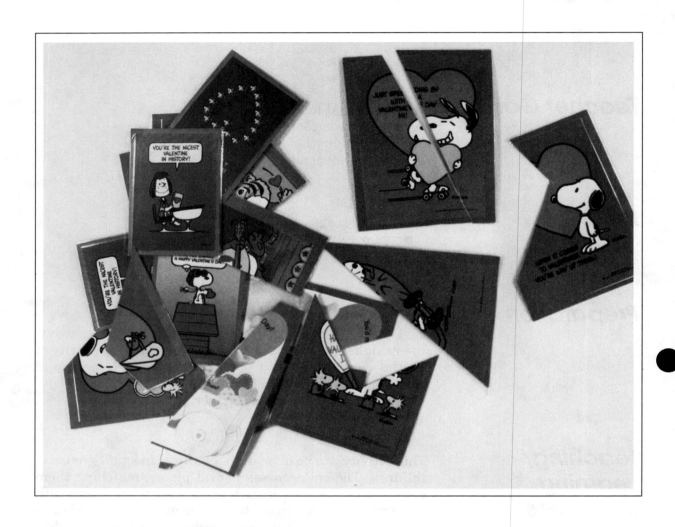

| **Interest Areas** | small motor |
| | language arts |

Themes

Valentine's day
friendship
paper
puzzles

Teacher Goals

promote visual-discrimination skills
foster problem-solving skills
encourage eye-hand coordination
promote esthetic appreciation

Materials

For each puzzle:
1 red or pink piece of tagboard, 4 1/2" x 6"
1 valentine card
glue or rubber cement
scissors
clear contact paper or laminate

Preparation

1. Glue a valentine card onto each tagboard piece.
2. Cut each puzzle in half, horizontally or vertically, creating varied cutting patterns—zigzag, wavy, or straight edge. The complexity of the cutting patterns should suit the developmental level of the children.
3. Cover all puzzle pieces with clear contact paper or laminate.

Teaching/ Learning Strategies

To promote learning as an interactive process, place the puzzle pieces on a table or the floor for use during self-directed play periods. If needed, encourage the children to locate the matching halves of the puzzles. Children may elect to participate individually or in small groups. This learning activity could be adapted for other holidays, such as Easter, Halloween, Thanksgiving, St. Patrick's Day, Christmas, and Hanukkah.

Leaf Concentration Game

| **Interest Areas** | small motor |
| | math |

Themes

counting
numbers
fall
trees

Teacher Goals

foster number-identification skills
promote counting skills
promote group cooperation
provide opportunities for following directions

Materials

yellow construction paper
orange construction paper
leaf stickers
black felt-tip marker
rubber cement or glue
clear contact paper or laminate

Preparation

1. Trace and cut out 1/2" x 8 1/2" leaves from the yellow and orange construction paper. (The number prepared will depend on the developmental level of the children.)
2. Print a sequence of individual numbers, beginning with 1 on the yellow leaves.
3. On the individual orange leaves, attach leaf stickers to correspond with the numbers on the yellow leaves.
4. Cover all pieces with clear contact paper or laminate.

Teaching/ Learning Strategies

The concentration game can be placed in a game, small-motor, or science center. To play the game, place all leaves facedown on a table or the floor. The first child turns over a yellow and an orange card. If the cards match, the child continues turning over cards until no match is made. When this happens, the child turns the cards facedown, and the next child takes a turn. The game is completed when all the matches have been made.

Wrapping-Paper
Lotto Game

| **Interest Areas** | small motor |
| | language arts |

Themes

paper
games
symbols

Teacher Goals

foster visual-discrimination skills
promote eye-hand coordination
foster group cooperation

Materials

4 pieces of yellow tagboard, 9" x 9"
35 pieces of yellow tagboard, 3"x 3"
black felt-tip marker
38 different patterns of wrapping paper
scissors
ruler
glue
clear contact paper or laminate

Preparation

1. To prepare the game boards, use a ruler and marker to divide each of the 9" x 9" pieces of tagboard into thirds, horizontally and vertically, creating nine equal squares.
2. Cut and glue a different wrapping-paper pattern onto each space of the game boards and glue the matching pieces onto each of the thirty-five tagboard cards.
3. Cover all of the pieces with clear contact paper or laminate.

Teaching/ Learning Strategies

This activity would make an excellent addition to the game center or the small-motor area of the classroom. The children may enjoy playing the game individually, with another child or teacher, or in small groups of three or four children. Provide each child with a game board. Place all player cards facedown or in a pile. The children take turns drawing one card at a time and matching it to a space on their own or someone else's board. When one player has filled all the spaces on his or her game board, turn the cards facedown and begin again.

Sticker Dominoes

| **Interest Areas** | math |
| | small motor |

Themes

games
can be adapted to any theme

Teacher Goals

promote the development of small motor skills
provide opportunities for following directions
foster cooperation
provide opportunities for taking turns

Materials

1 sheet of colored tagboard
4 different sets of four stickers
scissors
black felt-tip marker
clear contact paper or laminate

Preparation

1. Cut the tagboard into thirty-two 6" x 3" pieces.
2. Divide each tagboard piece in half with a marker, to create two equal squares.
3. Place one sticker on each half of the tagboard. Like dominoes, mix up the sticker combinations on each tagboard piece.
4. Cover all pieces with clear contact paper or laminate.

Teaching/ Learning Strategies

Place this activity in the game center or on a table in the small-motor area for use during self-directed play. The object of the game is to match stickers (see photograph). Some children may need to be guided by an adult to see possible solutions.

Lacing Cards

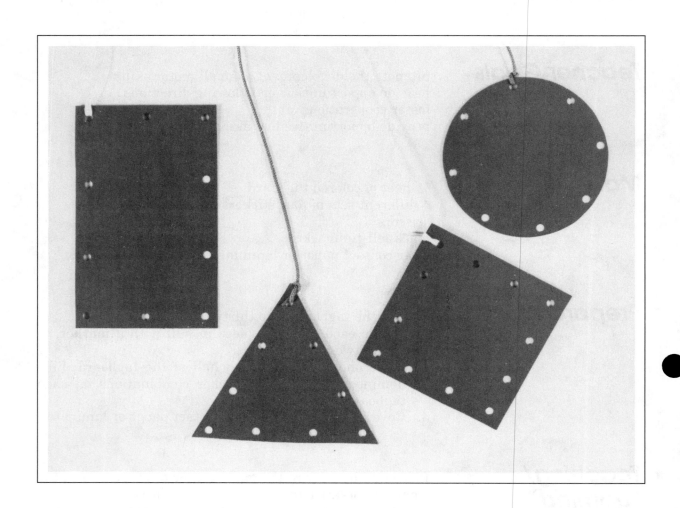

Interest Areas	small motor
	math
Themes	shapes
	colors
Teacher Goals	promote small motor skills
	foster eye-hand coordination
	encourage shape-recognition skills
Materials	1 sheet of tagboard
	shoestrings
	paper punch
	clear contact paper or laminate

Preparation

1. Trace and cut desired shapes or patterns for lacing cards (see photograph).
2. Use the paper punch to make holes around the perimeter of each card. Adjust the space between the holes to the developmental level of the children. When preparing cards for older children, space the holes closer together.
3. Cover the cards with clear contact paper or laminate.
4. Punch the circles again to remove the contact paper or laminate.
5. Tie a shoe string around one hole.

Teaching/ Learning Strategies

The lacing cards, like many of the activities in this book, should be used during self-directed play. The children may work individually or in small informal groups with the materials. For variety, two cards can be laced together.

Rainbow-Chain Chart

Make a rainbow chain.

1.
2.
3.
4.
5.
6.

Interest Areas	small motor
	math
	language arts
	social studies

Themes	colors
	patterns
	seasons
	rainbows
	holidays
	paper

Teacher Goals	promote group cooperation
	foster color-recognition skills
	nurture sequencing skills
	promote eye-hand coordination
	promote the development of small motor skills

Materials	1 sheet of tagboard, 22" x 28"
	colored felt-tip markers
	clear contact paper or laminate

Preparation

1. On the sheet of tagboard, use the markers to print the instructions and draw the corresponding illustrations.

Rainbow Chain

a. To make a rainbow chain, you need red, orange, yellow, green, blue, and purple strips of construction paper, 1" x 8".

b. Form a circle with a red strip of paper. Glue, tape, or staple the ends together.

c. Insert an orange strip through the red link and fasten.

d. Insert a yellow strip through the orange link and fasten.

e. Insert a green strip through the yellow link and fasten.

f. Insert a blue strip through the green link and fasten.

g. Insert a purple strip through the blue link and fasten.

2. Cover the tagboard with clear contact paper or laminate.

Note: For variety, the chains can be adapted to seasonal or holiday colors: In the fall, use red, orange, brown, and yellow; for Christmas, use red and white.

Teaching/ Learning Strategies

Gather the materials needed to make the rainbow chains. Display the chart at the children's eye level. Place the colored strips and the glue, tape, or staples in front of the chart. The children may work individually or in small groups during self-directed play periods. Some children may elect to repeat patterns to create chains of various lengths. The chains can be used to decorate a bulletin board, classroom door, children's lockers, or a particular area of the classroom.

Snowflake Chart

Interest Areas	small motor
	art

Themes

winter
weather
paper
scissors

Teacher Goals

foster eye-hand coordination
promote the development of small motor skills
promote self-esteem
promote esthetic appreciation
provide opportunities for following directions

Materials

1 sheet of light-blue tagboard, 6 pieces of white construction
    paper, 5" x 5"
black felt-tip marker
ruler
glue or rubber cement
clear contact paper or laminate

Preparation

1. Print the words "Make a Snowflake" across the top of the tagboard sheet.
2. Using a ruler and black felt-tip marker, draw six 11" x 8" rectangles on the remaining space of the tagboard (see photograph).
3. Sequentially number each rectangle as illustrated.
4. In the first rectangle, glue one of the white squares.
5. For the second rectangle, fold one of the white squares in half. Glue one half to the tagboard.
6. Fold another white square in half vertically. You will then have a rectangle. Fold up the bottom third and glue the back to the third rectangle so the last fold shows.
7. Take another white square and repeat the folds in steps 5 and 6. Then fold down the top third and glue the back to the fourth rectangle.
8. Take another square and repeat the folds in steps 5, 6, and 7. Cut this piece with scissors as you would to make a snowflake and glue it, still folded, to the fifth rectangle.
9. Take the last square and repeat the folds in steps 5, 6, and 7 and make the cuts as outlined in step 8. Unfold the completed snowflake and glue it to the sixth rectangle.

Teaching/ Learning Strategies

Self-directed art activities should be provided in the daily curriculum. Display the snowflake chart in the art area along with paper and child-size scissors.

Social
Studies

Birthday Crowns

Interest Areas

social studies

Themes

celebration
birthdays

Teacher Goals

promote self-esteem
encourage number-recognition skills
promote name-identification skills
introduce social-study concepts through a meaningful
   experience
provide a print-rich environment
promote visual-discrimination skills

Materials

construction paper in an assortment of colors
colored felt-tip markers
scissors
glitter
glue

Preparation

1. Trace and cut a crown pattern from construction paper.
2. Decorate the crown, using glitter and markers.
3. Print the child's name and age on the birthday crown.

Teaching/ Learning Strategies

If desired, the birthday child could choose the color of crown preferred. Older children may even enjoy decorating their own crown, as well as printing their name on it. Allow the child to wear the crown on his or her birthday. During snack, lunch, or group time, sing "Happy Birthday" to the child.

Note: Not all families celebrate birthdays. As a result, teachers need to be aware of individual families' beliefs and wishes.

Community-Helpers
Body Puppets

Interest Areas	social studies
	language arts
	dramatic play

Themes	puppets
	community helpers
	occupations

Teacher Goals	encourage creative expression
	promote language development
	introduce social-study concepts through a meaningful experience
	foster role-playing skills
	promote social skills
	enhance self-esteem

Materials	sheets of tagboard
	scissors
	colored felt-tip markers
	craft knife
	clear contact paper or laminate

Preparation

1. Draw a picture of a community helper, such as a firefighter or police officer, on the tagboard. If necessary, use an opaque projector to reflect a coloring-book image onto the tagboard, which you can then trace and cut out.
2. Color in the picture with felt-tip markers.
3. Cut holes from the tagboard puppet, large enough for a child's face and hands (see photograph).
4. Cover the puppet with clear contact paper or laminate.
5. Using a craft knife, cut away the contact paper or laminate from the holes.

Teaching/Learning Strategies

The puppets make an interesting addition to the dramatic-play or language-arts center. The children can insert their head and hands through the puppet holes. If available, provide a mirror for the children to observe themselves while they are wearing the body puppets.

"The Farmer in the Dell" Game Pieces

| **Interest Areas** | social studies |
| | music |

Themes

farms
occupations
games
music

Teacher Goals

promote cooperation
foster music appreciation
provide opportunities for taking turns
encourage group participation

Materials

1 sheet of white tagboard
colored felt-tip markers
scissors
yarn
paper punch
clear contact paper or laminate

Preparation

1. On the tagboard sheet, draw the figures from "The Farmer in the Dell"—a piece of cheese, a mouse, a cat, a dog, a nurse, a child, a farmer, and a spouse (see photograph).
2. Decorate the figures as desired with felt-tip markers.
3. Cut out the pieces with scissors.
4. Cover each piece with clear contact paper or laminate.
5. Punch two holes near the top of each tagboard figure. Cut a length of yarn that is long enough to fit over a child's head and string it through the holes and tie.

Teaching/ Learning Strategies

Use the game pieces while playing "The Farmer in the Dell." As each character is introduced, choose a child and place the appropriate game piece over his or her head. Afterwards, put the game pieces in an area of the classroom for use during self-directed play periods.

"The Goblin in the Dark" Game Pieces

Interest Area	social studies
Themes	Halloween
	games

Teacher Goals

provide opportunities for following directions
promote group cooperation
stimulate language skills
facilitate group participation
introduce traditional Halloween symbols

Materials

1 piece of orange tagboard, 8 1/2" x 9"
1 piece of black tagboard, 8" x 7"
1 piece of black tagboard, 8 1/2" x 6"
1 piece of white tagboard, 6" x 10"
1 piece of white tagboard, 8 1/2" x 11"
1 piece of green tagboard, 7" x 10"
colored construction paper
yarn
colored felt-tip markers
scissors
glue
paper punch
clear contact paper or laminate

Preparation

1. Trace and cut a figure representing a pumpkin, a bat, a cat, a ghost, a witch, and a goblin, from the tagboard.
2. Add details and decorate each figure with felt-tip markers and construction paper (see photograph).
3. Cover all pieces with clear contact paper or laminate.
4. Punch two holes near the top of each tagboard figure. Cut a length of yarn that is long enough to fit over a child's head and string it through the holes and tie.

Teaching/ Learning Strategies

This game can be played to the tune and directions of "The Farmer in the Dell." Continue singing the verses until each child has had a turn to represent a figure. Place the game pieces in an area of the classroom for use during self-directed play periods.

The Goblin in the Dark

1. The goblin in the dark
    The goblin in the dark,
    Hi ho on Halloween,
    The goblin in the dark.
2. The goblin takes a witch . . .
3. The witch takes a cat . . .
4. The cat takes a bat . . .
5. The bat takes a ghost . . .
6. The ghost takes a pumpkin . . .
7. The pumpkin stands alone,
    The pumpkin stands alone,
    Hi ho on Halloween,
    The pumpkin stands alone.

Farm Lotto Game

Interest Areas

social studies
small motor
language arts

Themes

farms
animals
occupations
games

Teacher Goals

promote visual-discrimination skills
foster eye-hand coordination
promote group cooperation

Materials

4 sheets of tagboard, 5" x 8"
24 pieces of tagboard, 2 1/2" x 2 1/2"
black felt-tip marker
scissors
ruler
24 pictures—2 of each—of farm items or animals cut from wrapping paper
clear contact paper or laminate

Preparation

1. With the felt-tip marker, divide each tagboard piece in half vertically and in thirds horizontally to create six spaces of equal size, 2 1/2" x 2 1/2" (see photograph).
2. Cut the remaining space on the tagboard piece to represent a roof of a barn.
3. Glue different pictures onto each space on the game boards and glue the matching pieces onto the twenty-four tagboard cards.
4. Cover all pieces with clear contact paper or laminate.

Teaching/ Learning Strategies

This activity can be played in groups of two to four children or one child and an adult. Provide each child with a game board. Place all player cards facedown or in a pile. The children take turns drawing one card at a time and matching it to a space on their own or someone else's board. When one player has filled all the spaces on his or her game board, turn the cards facedown and begin again.

Helper Chart

Interest Areas

social studies
language arts

Themes

I'm me, I'm special

Teacher Goals

foster group participation
promote an awareness of classroom tasks
promote an understanding that all living things need care
  and attention
encourage cooperation

Materials

1 sheet of yellow tagboard
construction paper
black felt-tip marker
pieces of tagboard, 7" x 2 1/2"
pictures of classroom tasks cut from magazines (optional)
scissors
glue
clear contact paper or laminate

Preparation

1. Print the words "Helper Chart" across the top of the
   tagboard sheet (see photograph).
2. Draw two horizontal lines and two vertical lines to make
   six 9" x 9" squares on the tagboard.
3. In each square, draw or paste a picture representing a
   classroom task—watering a plant, holding a door open,
   feeding the fish, setting the table, feeding the gerbils,
   marking the calendar, etc.
4. Below each picture, draw a 7" x 2 1/2" rectangle.
5. Cover all pieces with clear contact paper or laminate.
6. Prepare a name card for each child from the 7" x 1 1/2"
   pieces of tagboard.

Teaching/ Learning Strategies

Use tape or adhesive putty to attach the name cars to the
chart. Depending on teacher preference, the helpers names
can be changed on a daily or weekly basis. It is important,
however, to rotate the tasks evenly, providing each child an
opportunity to participate. This teaching aid is another
means of teaching the children how the printed word and
symbols are an important means of communication.
Consequently, this type of activity helps promote literacy.

Road Map for Small Cars and Trucks

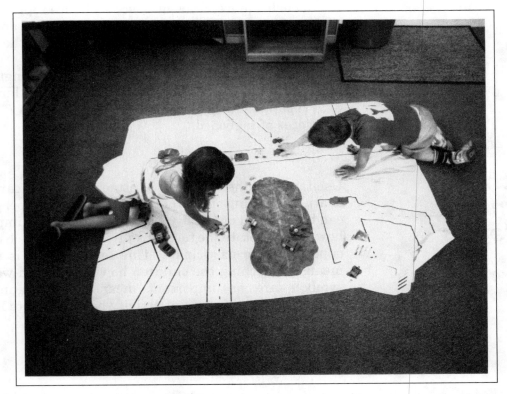

| **Interest Areas** | social studies |
| | small motor |

Themes

transportation
cars and trucks
wheels

Teacher Goals

promote cooperation
promote the development of small motor skills
encourage individual choice

Materials

1 piece of oilcloth or sheet of vinyl, 52" x 70"
colored, permanent felt-tip markers
ruler

Preparation

1. Spread the oilcloth on a large flat surface, such as a table or the floor.
2. Using felt-tip markers and a ruler, draw lines representing roads (see photograph).
3. Draw a pond and trees, if desired.

Teaching/ Learning Strategies

Place the road map on the floor in an open area with small cars and trucks. The children can "drive" the cars and trucks over the roads on the map.

Traffic Light

Interest Areas	social studies
	dramatic play

Themes

transportation
colors
shapes
safety

Teacher Goals

promote color-identification skills
stimulate language skills
promote shape-identification skills
introduce the concept of traffic signs
encourage safety awareness

Materials

1 sheet of blue tagboard
1 red, 1 yellow, and 1 green piece of acetate or cellophane
    paper
rubber cement or glue
masking tape
scissors
craft knife
clear contact paper or laminate

Preparation

1. Trace and cut the outline of a traffic-light from the sheet of tagboard.
2. From the traffic light, cut out three circles—one for each of the colored lights.
3. Cover the traffic light and pieces of acetate with clear contact paper or laminate
4. Using a craft knife, remove the contact paper from the circles of the traffic light.
5. Glue the appropriate-color acetate to the back of each circle, using rubber cement and masking tape.

Teaching/ Learning Strategies

Children learn safety rules through playful interaction with people and objects. Consequently, the traffic light should increase the children's awareness of their world. The adult should facilitate their involvement by pointing out the order of the colors and explaining the action that each color represents. The adult may also wish to shine a flashlight behind the colors of the traffic light. This aid could also be used as a prop in the outdoor play yard for trikes, scooters, and running games.

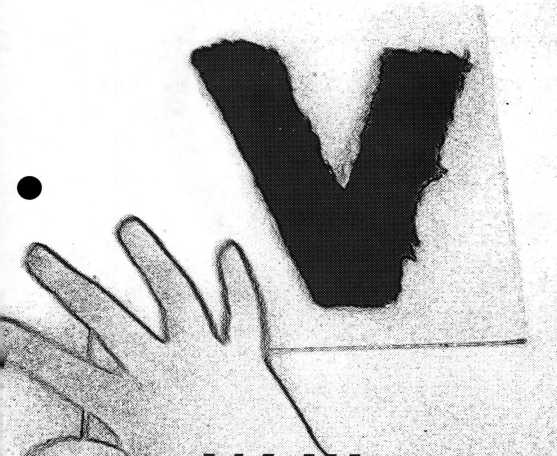

Writing Center

"The Apple Tree" Chart

Interest Areas	writing center
	language arts
	room environment

Themes

letters
symbols
apples
fruits
foods
rhymes and poetry

Teacher Goals

create a print-rich environment
foster reading-readiness skills
promote left-to-right progression skills
encourage the enjoyment of books
foster word-object identification skills

Materials

1 sheet of red tagboard
1 sheet of manila construction paper
scraps of green and brown construction paper
black, red, green, and brown felt-tip markers
rubber cement
clear contact paper or laminate

Preparation

1. Trace and cut a large apple out of the red tagboard.
2. Trace and cut a stem and leaf out of the construction paper and attach them to the apple with rubber cement (see photograph).
3. Trace and cut an apple out of the manila paper, approximately 1 1/2" smaller in diameter than the red tagboard apple.
4. Print the words of "The Apple Tree" poem on the white apple and draw symbols for the words "apple," "tree," "up," and "down," as illustrated in the photograph.

The Apple Tree

Way up high in the apple tree
Two little apples smiled at me.
I shook that tree as hard as I could.
Down came the apples. M'm were they good.

5. Color in the symbols with felt-tip markers.
6. Attach the white apple to the red with rubber cement.
7. Cover the chart with clear contact paper or laminate.

Teaching/ Learning Strategies

Hang the chart on a wall in the writing center at the children's eye level. Set up the chart for group time to introduce the poem. Use gestures to act out the poem. Older children may enjoy discussing the rhyming words.

"A Chubby Little Snowman" Chart

Interest Areas

writing center
language arts

Themes

winter
symbols
letters
communication
rhymes and poetry

Teacher Goals

promote an enjoyment of poetry
increase an awareness of the printed word
provide a print-rich environment
facilitate visual-discrimination skills

Materials

2 sheets of manila or white tagboard
colored felt-tip markers
clear contact paper or laminate

Preparation

1. Using felt-tip markers, print the words and draw the illustrations for "A Chubby Little Snowman" on two sheets of tagboard (see photograph).

A Chubby Little Snowman

A chubby little snowman had a carrot nose.
Along came a bunny, and what do you suppose?
That hungry little bunny, looking for his lunch,
Ate the snowman's carrot nose. Nibble, nibble, crunch.

2. Cut one of the tagboard sheets into sentence strips.
3. Cover the sheet of tagboard and the strips with clear contact paper or laminate.

Teaching/ Learning Strategies

Introduce the poem "A Chubby Little Snowman" with the chart during group time. Encourage the children to recite the poem with you. After this introduction, display the chart in the writing or language-arts center. Children can match individual sentence strips with the corresponding illustrations on the chart.

Alphabet Cards for Playdough

Interest Areas	writing center
	small motor
	language arts

Themes

letters
shapes
communication
books

Teacher Goals

promote letters-recognition skills
promote the development of small motor skills
foster eye-hand coordination
promote an interest in print

Materials

For the cards:
26 pieces of white construction paper, 9" x 12"
black felt-tip marker
clear contact paper or laminate

For the playdough:
water
salt
food coloring
oil
flour
alum

Preparation

1. On each piece of construction paper print an alphabet letter.
2. Cover all pieces with clear contact paper or laminate.
3. Prepare the playdough as follows:
   a. Combine and stir until dissolved 2 cups of water and 1/2 cup salt.
   b. If desired, add several drops of food coloring.
   c. Mix in 2 tablespoons of oil, 2 cups flour, and 2 tablespoons of alum.
   d. Knead five minutes until smooth.
   e. Store the playdough in an airtight container.

Teaching/ Learning Strategies

Place the cards and playdough at the writing center or in the art area. The daily schedule should allow many opportunities for the children to select their own activity.

Object-and-Word Cards

| **Interest Areas** | writing center |
| | language arts |

Themes

words
letters
paper
games
symbols

Teacher Goals

stimulate letter-recognition skills
foster word-object identification skills
encourage visual-discrimination skills
promote the development of language and literacy through
    a meaningful experience
contribute to a print-rich environment

Materials

pieces of light-colored tagboard, 7 1/2" x 6 1/2"
pieces of matching light-colored tagboard, 7" x 2 1/2"
colored felt-tip markers
scissors
clear contact paper or laminate

Preparation

1. Draw a picture of a common object in the top two-thirds
   of each 7 1/2" x 6 1/2" piece of tagboard (see photograph).
2. Using a black felt-tip marker, draw a line across the
   bottom of each tagboard piece and print the name of the
   object on the bottom third.
3. On one side of each 7 1/2" x 2 1/2" piece of tagboard, print
   the name of one object illustrated and written on the 7
   1/2" x 6 1/2" cards.
4. Turn each 7 1/2" x 2 1/2" card over and draw the object
   that corresponds to the name written on the opposite
   side.

**Teaching/
Learning
Strategies**

Place the object-and-word cards in the writing center.
Encourage children to identify and name the objects. Younger
children will be able to match the pictures of the objects. The
cards can also be displayed on the wall of the writing center
for children to practice their writing skills.

Wipe-off Cards

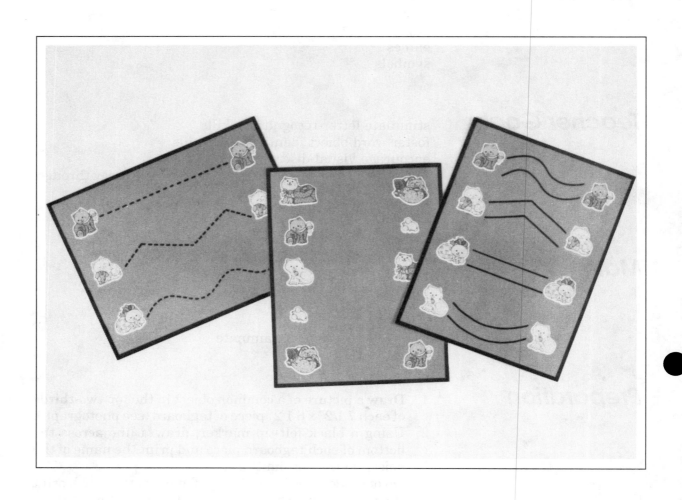

| **Interest Areas** | writing center |
| | small motor |

Themes

writing
writing tools
can be adapted to any theme

Teacher Goals

promote eye-hand coordination
promote the development of small motor skills
foster visual-discrimination skills

Materials

pieces of tagboard, 11" x 9"
stickers or hand-drawn symbols
black felt-tip marker
scissors
clear contact paper or laminate

Preparation

1. Attach a row of stickers to the left-hand side of a piece of tagboard (see photograph).
2. Attach identical stickers to the right-hand side of the tagboard in a different sequence.
3. Using the photograph as a guide, draw lines from one symbol to another.
4. Cover each card with clear contact paper or laminate.

Teaching/ Learning Strategies

This activity can be placed in the writing center. Display the cards and provide water color markers on a table in the writing or small-motor area. The object of the cards is to encourage the children to trace on or between the lines connecting the symbols. The cards can be cleaned by wiping with a damp cloth or paper towel.

Wipe-off Postcards

Interest Areas	writing center
	language arts
	small motor
	social studies
	dramatic play

Themes	communication
	letters and writing
	post office
	mail carriers
	friends
	vacations

Teacher Goals	foster small motor skills
	promote an awareness of print/letters
	encourage social skills
	promote the development of language and literacy through a meaningful experience
	provide a print-rich environment

Materials	pieces of tagboard, 6" x 9"
	ruler
	black felt-tip marker
	cancelled postage stamps
	glue or rubber cement
	clear contact paper or laminate

Preparation

1. Using a ruler and black marker, divide each tagboard piece in half vertically.
2. Draw three horizontal lines on the right half of the tagboard piece (see photograph).
3. Glue a cancelled postage stamp in the upper right-hand corner of the postcard.
4. Cover each postcard with clear contact paper or laminate.

Teaching/ Learning Strategies

Place the wipe-off postcards in the writing center, dramatic-play area, or on the small-motor table. Use watercolor markers to write or draw on the cards. Clean the cards with a damp cloth or paper towel.

Dried-Glue Rubbings

Interest Areas

writing center
language arts
small motor

Themes

shapes
letters
writing tools

Teacher Goals

foster tactile awareness
promote letter-recognition skills
foster shape-identification skills
introduce the difference between uppercase and lowercase
   letters

Materials

pieces of tagboard, 8" x 6"
glue

Preparation

1. Squeeze glue onto tagboard pieces in the form of letters
   or shapes.
2. Allow the glue to dry thoroughly.

Teaching/ Learning Strategies

Place the rubbings on a table in the writing or small-motor
center. Provide paper and large crayons. (Remove the paper
wrapper from the crayons for younger children.) If necessary,
demonstrate the process of placing a thin piece of paper over
the dried glue shapes. Then rub a crayon over the forms to
reveal the letters or shapes.

Tactile Letters

Interest Areas

writing center
language arts

Themes

letters
sounds
touch
communication
stores

Teacher Goals

encourage letter-identification skills
foster tactile awareness
provide an opportunity to see print in use
promote the development of small motor skills
provide more complex materials for the writing center

Materials

26 pieces of white or colored tagboard, 5" x 6"
textured fabric
scissors
rubber cement

Preparation

1. Cut the twenty-six alphabet letters from a piece of textured fabric.
2. Adhere each letter to a piece of tagboard, using rubber cement.
3. Allow pieces to dry thoroughly.

Teaching/ Learning Strategies

Children should be allowed to progress at their own pace in acquiring letter-recognition skills. Locate the tactile letters in the writing center. With older children, use the letters as a small-group activity; place them in a feely box, bag, or even pillowcase and ask the children to guess which letter they are feeling.

C
D
E
F
G
H
I
J
3
4
5
6
7
8